# TWO BLOCKS APART

### Juan Gonzales and Peter Quinn

**Edited by Charlotte Leon Mayerson**

**Photographs by the
Still Photography
Workshop
Harlem Youth
Unlimited**

**An Avon Library Book**

AVON BOOKS
A division of
The Hearst Corporation
959 Eighth Avenue
New York, New York 10019

First Avon Library Edition, November, 1966

To Robert Henry Mayerson

# Editor's Note

Juan Gonzales and Peter Quinn, two seventeen-year-old boys, live in the same New York City neighborhood. They are both high school seniors in the same school district, both Catholics in the same parish, both ballplayers with the same parks and school yards at their disposal. That they do not know each other is an urban commonplace; that they are utter strangers in the conditions of their lives, in their vision of what they themselves are, seems a personal illustration of the apparent failure of the American melting pot.

On another level, however, are the attitudes they share: first, a common devotion to their immediate families; then, a common unwillingness to "interfere" where any personal risk is involved; a common disinterest in spiritual matters; common misconceptions and resentments about parts of society other than their own. Perhaps, a clue to understanding "the next generation" lies as much in the similarities between these boys as in their differences, and what they say is revealing of each of them, quite apart from any comparison.

I know Juan and Peter as boys in the neighborhood. Peter, white, middle class, delivers clothes for the dry cleaner on the block. Juan, from a poor Puerto Rican family, runs errands for a local social service agency. In the course of our acquaintance I was struck by the ways in which each of them reacted to what we talked about, in what each considered important or worth considering, and in what conclusions they drew from the same life situations. Eventually, with their parents' permission, I began to record our talks. This book is based on conversations I have had with each of them separately. Put down on paper, the record becomes, in a very real sense, the memoirs of Juan Gonzales and of Peter Quinn.

The boys live two blocks apart, in two cultures separated by their social and economic conditions. Yet it would be a foolish oversimplification to explain all the differences between them, their estrangement, in this mechanical way. Obviously, each is an individual (and an adolescent individual at that) with a uniqueness more complex than the statistic of his class or race definition. Equally clear is that they both have been influenced, in various ways, by the larger world in which they have grown up.

The decision to consider these particular boys was not scientifically determined; they are typical only in that the objective facts of their lives are similar to those of many other urban boys of their backgrounds. Their names, identity, neighborhoods, and so on, have been disguised. The conversations have been edited to the extent that my own part of the talks has been omitted and the rest has been gathered together to make a continuing narrative within very loosely defined chapters. This arrangement has not changed the sense or context of the original material. No attempt has been made to "even up" the amount each boy says about any particular subject. (Juan is, most of the time, simply more talkative and ruminative than Peter, even when they're covering the same ground.)

The many almost inevitable psychoanalytic and sociological conclusions to be drawn from this material have been left to the reader. A few bare, descriptive facts about Juan and Peter may be helpful at the onset. Juan is six feet tall, taller than anyone in his family and taller than most of the boys he knows. He is slim, with light brown skin, compact features, and straight black hair, and he is meticulously groomed. He is a restless boy, who has trouble sitting still and he participates in every conversation with a notable intensity. He speaks with a Puerto Rican accent, in a mixture of slang and "big words" (many of which he seems to have picked up from a social worker in the neighborhood). He obviously enjoys a good story, and possibly, some of the things he talks about are more elaborate in the telling than in the occurrence.

Peter is fair, regular featured, five feet seven inches tall, with a rather stocky athletic build. He is a remarkably easygoing, cheerful youngster, full of the fun he so admires. His diction is excellent, his conversation casually phrased but deliberately considered.

Both boys are enormously likable. Each has moving human qualities and potentials for society—a society which does not

10

appear to have shown them yet how it may be served, or that it requires service at all.

(The photographs that accompany the text illustrate situations similar to what Juan and Peter discuss, though neither the boys nor their real surroundings are shown. The pictures were taken by five teen-agers: Samuel Roberts, Arthur Lobo, Ray Mills, Rodney Smith, and Sandra Smith, students of the Still Photography Workshop of Harlem Youth Unlimited. "Haryou," a publicly supported Harlem youth organization, supplied them with cameras, equipment, and technical instruction. The art and sensitivity of the work was provided by the young people themselves.)

# Family

Juan has two older sisters. One remained in
Puerto Rico with her grandmother when the
family migrated to New York about ten years
ago. The other sister, recently married,
frequently visits and spends the night in her
family's home. Juan's brother is fifteen, two
years younger than Juan, and he lives at home.
Their mother left the children's father, a
part-time day laborer, when she came to New
York. She has subsequently remarried a much
younger man. The children rarely see their
father. When Juan talks about "Welfare," he
means public assistance from the New York
Department of Welfare.

Peter is the youngest of four children in a
very close and stable Irish Catholic family. His
father is vice president in charge of sales
in a large industrial concern. His brother is
twenty-six and a salesman in a firm in his
father's industry. One sister is twenty-two,
a recent college graduate. Another sister, three
years older than Peter, died of leukemia
several years ago. The Quinns bear a strong
resemblance, with Peter and his brother looking
particularly alike. The "club" to which Peter
refers is a well-known, rather exclusive private
New York club to which his father belongs.

# Juan Gonzales

My family is very close and we try to help each other. Like my brother is about fifteen now, but he doesn't think like me, on his own. I've been trying to get him out of the gang, but he's been sticking with it up to now. Well, he doesn't know it, but I brought over a boy that I know and I introduced him to my brother and now they kind of hang out together and they're friends and it's nice. They don't stay with that crowd. They don't go around smoking pot or beating up little boys and that's what I want.

I think sometimes my little brother has it tough because of the way the other kids think about *me*. Not belonging any more to a gang and all that. But it doesn't matter. You see, my brother, like if they tell him to take a drink, he doesn't know it's going to get him into trouble. They say, "Let's go and beat up some little kid." He might just do it. Or smoke pot. But I think now I got a start in breaking him away.

My one sister is nineteen. You know, everybody thought she was going to turn out wrong. She was very popular in school, but she didn't like school because she just didn't get it. She wanted to go out all the time and my mother just kept her close in the house, cooking and cleaning, you know. Then she married this nice, old-fashioned guy and they live good together. She's got a little baby and they are doing all right. The only thing is, now she and the baby have to stay with us for a while. It's kind of crowded and the Housing, they don't know about it so far. But my sister was afraid in her own house. Somebody came in and robbed them. Twice, three times that happened and she won't stay there any more.

My other sister—she's about twenty-one—she would never come here to New York. She's in Puerto Rico with my grandmother and my mother can't get her away. It seems dumb, but I've got to say that so far she's the only one of us to graduate from high school.

I haven't been to Puerto Rico since I left when I was six, but I remember what it was like there. It was like being in a mudhole and you can't get out until someone who likes you—that's my mother—pulls you out of there and gets you a decent place to live. That's the way I feel about Puerto Rico.

My family talks about going back, but they say things like they don't want to go back there now, not until they get enough money to start a business of their own, and all this. But I know they'll never go back because I can tell that they prefer living here under these circumstances than going back and working for a lousy fifty cents an hour.

They think it was better there because it was sort of like a country of their own, but now it wouldn't be the same. Now you've got all kinds of people there, colored and whites, the same troubles as here. Before, it was all Puerto Rican, so when a Puerto Rican came from the United States with a lot of money, he felt good. I mean, he felt like a middle-class person and he felt that he was still in his own group. There was no discrimination against him. Now he doesn't feel the same.

I'd never go back anyhow. All I can remember about San Juan was the mud. Mud, yeah, that's all there was. We lived in a place called Fangito—that would be like a little mudhole in Spanish, and that's what it was. There was disease all over the place. The water was contaminated I think and we were always rolling in the mud. No matter where you walked, you were in the mud.

The shacks, the houses we had, were hot in summer and cold in the winter. And if someone came in to rob you, man, although you had close neighbors, nobody bothered to come up. You know, they had their own problems. That's the way it was.

I haven't ever been back. I've seen pictures of it and I've heard about it and everybody tells me it is a wonderful place, that I should have stayed there. I answer them and I tell them to go to hell because I wasn't ever going to stay in that place.

Even though I was so small I remember Puerto Rico. Mostly I remember my father. He and his brother used to drink and they used to fight and they used to come home and leave the bottles hanging around. And you know, the whiskey bottles were there without anybody watching them and I tampered with them sometimes. But I guess we were kind of lucky, my brother and sisters and me. We didn't go into any of that drunk stuff because my mother never drank or let us near it.

But the rest of them, the family, all of them were always drunk. I remember my grandfather, my father's father, he was so mean. Whenever you did something, anything, he thought you were doing wrong. And we lived in this house with them and everybody used to get hit. My mother was the youngest in the family and she used to get beat up all the time. By everybody. I mean, you know, no matter who.

Well, she finally got fed up and even though it meant leaving us for a while, she went to the United States and we kids were there. We had to stay in my father's father's house and *there* we had a *nice* time. Every time we got up in the morning until we got to bed at night we were either beat up or cursed at or something like that. My father hardly stayed at home. He was always drinking and fooling around with other women. He thought himself a playboy. He's sort of ridiculous, you know, an old man going out there trying to prove he's young.

I found out, then and there, from where I've been and how the people act, I found out that most Puerto Ricans like to drink, especially the men. And they usually hit their wives. Whereas I consider the wife something precious. You don't hit your wife; you talk to her, you make love to her, or whatever you do, you don't hit her. Maybe I'm premature about this thing. I don't know, but I think you don't go hitting a woman just because she maybe doesn't do something the way you like.

Take my grandfather. My grandfather didn't do nothing for a living. His children were working for him. He beat everybody up and everybody grew up to hate him.

And even my mother's family. In a way, it was like living in an early age, sort of like when the United States was fighting the Indians. These people, they believed in all kinds of crazy cures and crazy ways of bringing up their children. Like if you couldn't swim, they'd throw you in the lake or something. If you drowned, that was your tough luck. They never stopped to think that they could—you know—hold on to you and give you a guide and show you how to swim.

Everybody down there was so much savage in a way. I am not trying to say that my family was savages. All I'm saying is that they didn't know how to act. They didn't communicate civilized. They didn't talk back and forth like other people do. They would fight, they would argue, and whoever was stronger would win. And that's who would rule in that family household or outside. If you couldn't handle yourself, even when you were real small, that was your tough luck.

But now it's different. Like my mother, you know, she's been through it. Before, she would yell all the time, yell and scream and hit us. But now, no fights, no arguments.

Like it's the atmosphere. I mean, you're not talking the way you were before because the past couple of years you don't have to fight against anybody else for your food. You can do it on your own. And this way, you feel more reliable, like to yourself and to others.

My mother even got to be a floor lady. She had studied from nothing, I mean, working on a sewing machine she didn't even know how to operate and now she can take a machine apart and put it back together and she knows all types of different machines. She was a floor lady for a long time, so now she knows that wherever she goes in New York, if anything goes wrong on us, she can always find a job. In Puerto Rico, what can she do?

And I think she's happier now. She can find—well—other people wouldn't, but what we would call the luxuries. And what can you get over there? Only mud and screaming and being beaten up.

You know, it is a funny thing about my family. My father wasn't ever really with us. Since I came to New York, my father has never been with us. My mother divorced him after we got here and that was it. He went his way and I went mine—we went ours. He was supposed to pay alimony and he was paying fifteen dollars I think. As the years grew, went by, he started to slow the payments and then didn't want to pay at all because we were getting a little older. And it stated right there that he had to pay until we were eighteen. My little brother is only fifteen and he hasn't paid for over a year now. But we don't bother with him.

I used to see him. My mother wanted us to see him because they—my mother and my stepfather—they wanted us to know our real father. But I stopped seeing him. First of all, I didn't like him because I remembered what he had done to me and my sisters and my little brother and my mother in Puerto Rico. Down there, my mother would be slaving over the stove and we would be outside playing in the mud or something. Then he'd come in drunk. He'd start beating *her* up. She would be crying and then he'd come at us and he would beat us up. And this went on for a long time, until my mother couldn't take it any more.

I tell you, we couldn't take it any more either. I started getting a little older and a little fatter and my father used to grab me by the hand and throw me against the wall and I used to have a lot of trouble. I broke three of my bones right here on my arm and one on my chest. When he threw me against the wall one day I didn't land on my back, I landed on my chest. And my mother had to take me to the hospital. We were lucky because they were giving out medicine and things like that, but they weren't charging too much. Some of the things were even free.

Anyway—my father. My father. My *real* father. I don't know what job he had in Puerto Rico. I don't really know. But here he was a dry cleaner. You know, a guy that presses suits and shirts and things like that. I remember one day, about three or four years ago, he came to my house and my mother asked him for the alimony money. He didn't have it and my mother told him he better start paying up or she was going to take him to court. Well when she said that, he started getting wild, you know, going haywire.

My mother was remarried by then, but her husband was working and my real father had just come along for a visit. Well, I was in the other room when I heard that screaming and yelling and all that, and I came in and I told him to get out. All of a sudden, just like that.

I know I should respect my father, but I have no respect for him at all. I told him to get out or else I would throw him out and I was pretty big by then. I was ready to do it. My father, my real father, he cursed at me and he said to my mother, "Is this what you bring up?" And I said to him, I looked right at him, and I said, "At least she stays."

Then he started walking out nice and slow, you know, like a little kid who wants to prove that he's not afraid. I was so riled up at him, when he was only halfway to the door, watching him walk so slow and so mean. I slammed the door and I told him that I don't want him here. And my mother said that she didn't want him there either.

But I don't know, he never showed up again, and then I haven't seen him for such a long time. I heard that he had married again to a nice woman. But we don't see any of my father's relatives any more. Not his brothers or his sisters because they are all the same way. My name is Gonzales and that is their name, but it doesn't mean anything to me. His sisters, they all talk and talk. They used to bring a lot of problems and they would get you so involved that you couldn't find a way out. And when I used to go to their house, their husbands were always beating up their wives because that's the way they are. And my father's brothers, they were always on the mean side. They always wanted sex and they always wanted money and they didn't give a heck how they got it. One of them is a crook and another's a dope addict. He spent half his lifetime in jail. He's still in jail now.

Another one was a nice guy, but he likes his kids to drink and they are not even in their teens yet. He likes to show them how to be old before their time and that's what I think happened to me. That's how come I grew up too fast.

My father did the same thing. He made me. When you lose your father, by divorce or by death or by anything like that, you start big. You know you are alone.

Your mother, how long can she last? And how long can she work for you? How do you keep up with things when she is too old or sick or she is out of work? What are you going to do for the rent? I thought of that when I was about seven and I thought: When am I going to start to work? Things like that.

It was like that when we first came here, after my mother

sent for us from Puerto Rico. We weren't having so much fun then. Business conditions were bad and my mother wasn't working. She'd been laid off. That was a bad time because we were ready to shoe on. We were ready to be thrown out of the house and we weren't living anywhere. We were like you call the peasants of the pack.

But we never took from Welfare. We felt kind of—you know—with pride. We were like alone. And while my mother was looking for work I was doing some shoe shining on the side and my sister and little brother were going to school. I think I was about eight then. I was going to school too, but I would play hooky most of the time. I was surprised when I found out I was passing in all my grades anyhow.

I was making enough money then to provide sort of like what we couldn't do without. You know, when my mother didn't have enough or she needed a couple of dollars, I would have it. And usually I would take care of my little brother and my sister by this shoe shining thing. I mean, if my mother's working and there's no money for something, I would have the money to go down the stairs and buy them something to eat.

Boy! I know what it feels like to be hungry. You watch somebody eat downstairs or you see him walk by with ice cream and it drops on the floor or something. You feel like killing the person, you know, letting all that food go to waste.

And the neighbors, they couldn't help. They were worse off than we were. Their kids were out for themselves. Whenever they'd get food, they ate it up like as if it was no end to it and whatever was left they would throw away. They wouldn't bother to take it home. They were like savages. I agree that we were on the same level as they were at the time. But when you are hungry, I mean, what can you do?

The rest of the family was having it rough, too. You have to remember that this was a bad time. People in factories were being laid off because they didn't have enough work for them. Our relatives were in the same boat that we were. Maybe they were a little better off. I mean, at least they had something to eat. But they couldn't spare anything for us.

All of us, my sister and my brother and my mother and

me, we all suffered. I mean when one ate, everybody ate, and when one didn't eat, the others didn't eat, too. It worked that way with us. Most of the food went to my mother because she was the one who was working. We kind of picked at the food so she would eat and be able to go to work. She had to come *back*. That's what we kids knew.

We didn't go for Welfare because—well—we consider it charity. I mean if it is a helping hand, you are going to pay it back, fine! You know, you may owe, but when someone tells you, "Here, I don't need it," you feel like "Man, don't give it to me just because you don't need it." If I need something I take it, but I don't think it's the same thing. Like the guy at the store, he would give us credit and that was fine. But as soon as he found out that we couldn't pay up, he stopped, and that was it. Then you had to pay every time you went for anything.

Once, a couple of my friends and me, we went around to that big bakery company that's out there on the street. Well, they had cookies coming in and out of that place, being baked, and bread and things like that. There is a big machine that's on a sort of belt and it passes by a small window that's like on a basement floor.

Well, we cracked open that window and as the breads were going by, we grabbed them and we put them into a bag.

I remember going home that day. It was real bitter out. Cold. And the package felt good, the bread was still warm, hot, under my shirt.

I got home that night and I had a shopping bag full of bread from going back and forth. I took it home and I put it on the table there, the bread all cut up like it was and then I ran out of the house because I didn't want my mother to know that I'd stolen it. Anyway, she must have known I had taken it from someplace. But we were starving. I mean, we weren't doing so well and she needed that bread for us and she never said anything to me. Then, someone really helped me, this guy named Manuel. He told me all the tricks of the trade of stealing, and it was just like giving me money once he showed me that I could do very good, stealing.

The only thing is, I never stole from another person. I

didn't want to do that. I mean, I never went into somebody's house and stole. And I never take enough to leave a poor guy bankrupt, you know, or take from a guy who can't afford it. I mean like once I was taking fruit from a market I worked in after school. That guy's two sons both had English racers, they have radios, they have TV's, they have everything. Son comes in, the father asks him how much he needs and he gives him five dollars. So I mean if I see that he gives him five dollars, then I can go and take little bits of fruit here and there.

That man was always watching you anyhow. Finally it got so they were watching me so much I felt like a crook. So I did the next best thing—I stole. Bill, the fruit-stand man, he let me take. It was sort of a private joke between him and me. You know, the boss telling him not to let me have any fruits, and me, walking off with them right to the back of his own store.

Then, when I was about nine, Manuel, the friend I had, showed me how to get stuff from a store. I would see something I'd want and put it under my shirt at first. But Manuel showed me how fast to move and other little tricks. Like you buy three or four cans of chicken soup. After you pay for it and you've got a receipt in your bag, what you do is to say, "Wait a minute, I forgot something." Then you go looking around and you start putting other things in your bag. You get back to the check-out and say, "No, nothing here I want," and then you walk out. But if they stop you, you got a receipt.

The good thing is that if you work in a team, you do better. Alone, they would be watching me. Then another thing: Manuel is very cool and calm. I mean he's something to see. Like, I always thought I was good at taking stuff, but the way he did it made me look like an amateur. And I studied from him for about a year.

One time, though, he did get caught. We were using the old trick of buying something and then going back and putting other things in. They had a floorwalker in that store and I spotted him. You see a guy and you watch him for a while and see that he's not buying anything, just watching people. Well, when I saw the setup, I said to Manuel, "Come on, man, they're going to catch you. There's a floorwalker over there!" Manuel was stealing candy bars and everything. He was stuffing things into his coat, into his sleeves, into his boot. I mean he had food everywhere. He didn't need all that junk, but it was just for getting back the old touch after a layoff.

Well, he wouldn't stop—and there's no code of ethics when you steal. I mean if he gets caught, I can walk out and leave him, just like he could leave me. Me, I really was shopping for my mother, so I started over to the counter, you know, checking out? And Manuel was going toward the door when the floorwalker called us over. "Oh, man!" I said to myself. "Oh, help! And my mother, wait till my mother hears about this!"

Well, it really turned out funny because the guy took us into the other room and he started checking me over. I said: "What are you doing, officer? Are you a policeman?" He says, "I'm a floorwalker. I was a policeman, but I'm walking this floor now." Well, I got this guy started giving us his life story. Then he said he thought he saw me take something, and I told him I only bought these things for my mother. He looked into the bag, saw a receipt, and the jerk didn't even check it. That's the good part about that trick, they never do.

He started looking at Manuel's coat and found a candy bar. Then he looked at me and said, "You'd better go, son." Son! I said to Manuel, "Well, how could you do it!" And that dumb cop says, "Well, you never know who you hang around with." I played it good. I looked at Manuel straight like, and I said, "My mother, she always thought you were such a nice boy." I went outside, but I was really dying of that joke.

Manuel came out a little while later with his boots in his hand, walking down the street in his socks. They'd had him in the back, beat him up, made him strip and took all his candy out. I asked Manuel why he was such a stupid crook and he said he was out of touch. It was his first time in a couple of weeks because he didn't have anybody to companion him. You know, like you don't really do it for the stealing, you do it to show your friend up. If I could get into a place easy and just take something, and I knew it was easy to get out, well I wouldn't touch it. But if I can walk in with guards all over the place, that's the time I would do my best.

We had a very clever play one time at that school down the block. We thought about it for a month before we went, and we really planned it. We went down and knocked on the side door, and when this woman answered the door, real polite I said, "Well, thank you. Can I use the lavatory?" I knew how that would work! She looked sort of embarrassed and said, "Sure," and walked right away. We went into the bathroom and opened the window a little bit.

Well, the next day was Sunday and we hung around until it was night and then we went back. There was the window, still open. It was real dark and nobody was around. We just pushed the window down more, climbed in, and fixed the window again. I was wearing sneakers, but that Manuel, he was wearing shoes and he went "squeak, squeak, *boom*," all the way down that black hall to the library. Well, that big room is wired for alarm, and we saw that right away with our flashlights. I said, "Man, it's crazy. We can't get in here." And I wanted to get out.

Well, after a while I cooled down and looked around. I figured that maybe one of those little windows at the top of the door was loose. So Manuel gave me a lift. I hit one of them and it opened. Then I dropped down and let him in. We turned on our flashlights and walked around and there were books, school supplies, and candy bars at like a counter they had there in front. We love candy—special treat. I think that's the most we took off that place, a pile of candy. But there were pens and pencils and paper—beautiful kind of paper, best paper I've ever seen, with green lines.

I took mostly school supplies because it was that time of the year, and I could use a lot, or sell it easy. And we figured if we steal money, they're going to be after us, or if we steal something very valuable, they'll be after us. Something that's not worth so much they'll be able to forget about in a few days. So we took candy and cigarettes, cartons of them.

And they had beautiful gold pens. The sign said they were ten dollars. Manuel and I were fighting over one of those pens for about half an hour. Here we are, in the middle of this place and everything to pick from, and we were fighting over one lousy pen. So what we did was we took all the paper, a couple of brief cases, notebook covers and thousands and thousands of pens, the kind that cost $1.50, $2.50. I left my stuff at Manuel's house because in mine there's no place to hide it. You walk in even with a pack of cigarettes you took, you could be seen by my mother.

But Manuel has a basement that you could hide thousands of things in it and never find them. Once, we even electrocuted a dog down there—by mistake. We were setting up some wires from one side to the other, like a burglar-alarm system, to protect our stuff. But it had no covering over it or anything, so when the dog decided to walk right past it, there was nothing we could do about it. After that we turned the wire off and forgot about that. We put the dog over to the side and covered him up. Couldn't do much for him anyway.

Manuel's away in the penitentiary now. Boy, when he was small, they'd bring him home everyday. He'd steal all the time, for kicks. He *had* to keep doing it. Me, I just do it whenever there's nothing doing or when I don't give a heck about anything. But I haven't done it much since I left Manuel two or three years ago.

All that time, we didn't see my real father. Who wanted to see him? Nobody needed him. He was supposed to give us money, but when he first came from Puerto Rico the court hadn't decided yet about the alimony and things like that. So we were a little worse off. Then, finally, my mother found work and they made him start paying alimony and we moved to the projects and everything started turning out better.

Then my mother married a new husband, my stepfather. He works in the Transit and he loves his job, meeting the people and all. He's very nice—young, and he's just so gay. He's like a buddy. He's not like a father. You know, I mean, he never asks us to do anything by force. He never hit us. We couldn't take that any more. You can only get beaten so far and then you have to come back, but we never even had any disagreements with him. If he only disagrees, he asks my mother to straighten us out. But he would never hit us.

And he talks to us, gives us advice, and most of his advice I've taken, and I've found out it's good advice. It helps me. He helps me as much as he can. Like my real father, ha!

But my mother is the one in this world that I count on. You see, I can do everything wrong. I can be the worst kind of person. I can kill somebody. But as long as I know my mother doesn't approve, I don't go near him, see? Because my mother's gone through a lot over these past years for us. And you want to pay her back, but you have no money or anything. You want to even her back some way of what she missed on her own parents and even from my real father.

Like times the cops pick you up and bring you home in a police car? The people that know me, they believe me that I didn't do anything, but the people that don't know me, they hear gossip. And you know what, that is the worst thing. The only reason I don't break out and start yelling at those people is because of my mother. Because she has to live there, you know. I don't want people to talk about *her* like she's raising a lunatic or something.

Because most of the time, my mother and me, we have an understanding. Once when I was about ten, what I did was to go off by myself because I didn't know how to scream you know, how to make out. My mother was mad at me for something I did and she started hollering at me and I didn't think it was right. So I went off by myself because, you know, if you start with them, they are going to really hit you.

I stayed around some ditches all night and about two o'clock I came home. My real father wasn't with us then and my mother didn't get married again yet. When I came into the house, nobody spoke to me. I went into the bathroom, washed my hands, my mother put the plate on the table, and I started to eat.

But then she started to cry and that made me feel *bad*. I didn't know why she was crying until my sister and my little brother got me in the room. They asked me why I ran away and I said, "Run away?"

My mother was listening at the door and then she knew

that I didn't run away and we had sort of an agreement. But I was always going out then. I never stayed home from the time I was about eight. I would come home and sometimes I would do my homework and then I'd run out. That was all right for me though. I mean my father wasn't there.

My parents have a lot of fun together. They're an ideal couple. They always have laughs between them, lots of fun. I don't expect to get married until I'm twenty-seven or twenty-eight, but when I do, I want what they have. I know them the best and I can see myself very well in a life like theirs.

I think it is really some experience to see your children grown up, to watch your boy become a man, see him get a job and become set up for the rest of his life. What a feeling that must be to them! My parents are very proud of my sister and my brother, now that they're on their own. And they're still waiting for me. That's what my father says, "Still waiting for you."

My father can be very strict when he wants to. In very clear-cut, very precise terms he lets us know what he expects. For example, the principal says that you should study at least two and a half to three hours a night, and my father sees that I do. Three hours a night for study, come in from the street by five thirty in the afternoon, be in bed by eleven during the week. At night I go into my room and he says, "Don't come out until three hours are up. And if you have more homework, don't come out then."

My father doesn't hit me much or spank me now that I'm grown. He kids around about it and says that now that I'm so big and with such a hard head, he might get hurt. But there are still some things that make him very angry. One of the things that he cannot stand is stupid mistakes without a good explanation. Once I had to pick up a pair of plane tickets for him and I forgot all about it. I walked around all morning and all afternoon with the twenty dollars in my pocket and just forgot all about the tickets. When I got home and he asked me about them, he was really angry. He just picked me right off the ground and threw me into the room. I must have been about thirteen or fourteen then; now, picking up tickets is one thing I do right away when I have to.

Another thing that gets my father angry lately is when he

sends me up to the store for something, to get bread and milk or do some shopping. He might say, "And please get the *Times* when you come back." So sometimes I might bring the bread and milk and the other food and forget the *Times*, or else I bring home the wrong newspaper. That gets my father furious and he calls me a stupid idiot. He says that I'm very smart and that I should use my brains and not do things like that.

But my father has explained to us what he wants for us and how he wants to help us grow up right. One night he took me into his room and we had a long talk and he told me that when he was eleven years old he used to hang out in an old shack with his friends. It was a place that older kids used and sometimes, when the little boys were playing there, they'd hear these bigger boys planning to rob a grocery store or something like that. My father said "Peter, I was really brought up with hoodlums, really bad ones. I know that there's nothing like that in your life now, but I don't ever want you to get anywhere near that, because it's a terrible life." Because of the hard time he had, my father always tells me to keep up, to pay attention to etiquette, to my studies. My father went to college, but it wasn't easy for him the way it will be for me. He had to work his way through Notre Dame and then, after he graduated, he got a good job. Now he's vice president of a very big and important company and really knows himself how to succeed and how to have a good life.

I don't understand this psychology or whatever it is. I don't understand that. Child psychology is no way to bring up children. You shouldn't do certain things because they're bad, and how is your boy going to understand? How are you going to teach a blind person what the color red looks like? I think that if I had a child, and he was playing with fire, I wouldn't tell him that it was bad in a quiet voice. You would really have to do something powerful to show him. Or else, I suppose, let him get burned. In a way, my father tries to protect us from getting burned by good discipline. Then the other side of this is that my father is always fair. I never resented even a spanking because whenever I got one, my parents were always sure that I needed it, that I'd really done something I needed to be straightened out about. I could see it myself.

Another thing about my father is that he hasn't taught us to be snobs, or to boast about what we have and other people don't have. When I was younger, I used to go to the Day Camp that my father's club runs, but I didn't like it at all. All the children with me were wealthy, more than comfortable. But those kids knew it and they took advantage of it. They considered that their fathers were very powerful, so if anything happened to them, or if the counselors tried to discipline them, they'd say, "Don't touch me or I'll tell my father."

I found it very annoying because my father didn't teach us to be like that even though he belonged to that club since he was twenty.

The nice thing about our family is that we all have the same taste. I have exactly the same taste as everybody else in my family, even when it comes to girls. When I want to take out a girl, I show her to them and they almost always approve. You see, before I take a girl out my father would have to—or not have to, but it would be nicer—if my father or my parents knew her parents. One of the things that I think is very important is that a girl have good diction and since it is also important to my family, there is never any problem. Another example is that my mother says if I go out with a girl who is chewing gum in public, it doesn't make a very good appearance. Well, she almost didn't have to tell me that because I don't enjoy being with a girl like that either. When I take out a girl, I don't want to feel superior to her, and you can't help feeling superior to a girl who is loud, or chewing gum, or using bad diction.

I met a girl at a school dance last year and I thought she was really beautiful. I came home that night and I told my parents that I'd met this nice girl who goes to Sacred Heart. Her name was Wanda. What a name! It almost scared my parents off. But I told them that she was really a beautiful girl and that she spoke beautifully. Well, I was telling my mother about her when my sister came in. Patty is a real tease, and I'm glad when I'm home alone with the dog and my father and without her. That night she looked at me and she said, "Well, you seem to have met a girl, huh, Casanova? What school does she go to?" I told her that Wanda goes to Sacred Heart and then

Patty asked me how her diction was. I answered, "Impeccable," and she was satisfied. The way that incident turned out was that I showed Wanda to my family at church the next Sunday, and they liked her very much and liked the way her family looked.

The girls we go out with in our clique are pretty much the girls from Holy Family, my elementary school. They're the same girls that have always been in our group and although once in a while we date other girls, mostly it's them. Of course, that doesn't include all of the girls we went to grammar school with. One of those went bad in about seventh grade. She began to smoke and completely changed. She was a wild girl, really gone astray from the time she was pretty young.

None of the girls that I go out with smoke or act like that. Generally we meet at the church dances or else we might have some private party, like recently I've been going to quite a few sweet-sixteen parties. The last one was a week ago. The girl's family rented a room at a hotel downtown and that was a very neat party. Or else next week some of us boys are going to give a party at one of my friend's houses. We'll have sandwiches and Cokes and pretzels and all the boys will chip in. Of course his parents will be home to chaperone, and we'll dance and talk and play games or shoot some pool on their pool table. When we were a lot younger, in eighth grade, we'd play kissing games and that sort of thing at parties, but not any more. Now all that has moved on to be more private.

I haven't had a party in my own house for about a year, but that was a good one. A lot of us were going off to a local dance, and we had a dinner party at our house beforehand. About ten boys and girls for dinner, with my parents.

Of course, when I go away to college, the system won't work out too well, and then I will date girls on my own. But, as I said, there's not going to be any conflict because my parents' taste is the same as my taste. It's the same way with drinking. My dad and my brother sometimes have a beer while they're watching the ball game on TV, or they might have a drink if somebody comes to visit, but they certainly never let me have any liquor. Once my brother had a gin and tonic in his hand and he was mixing it with a stirrer. When he wasn't looking,

I took the stirrer and tasted it and my mother saw me. She said that she knew the way to discourage me and she gave me a full glass of a lot of gin and a very small amount of tonic. I drank it, but I almost died of the way it tasted, and it really cured me. She did the right thing that time. Sometime, when I'm older, I would like to try to see what it feels like to get really drunk. But I'll wait until I'm a lot older and until my father says it's all right. Probably when I'm in college, maybe a sophomore.

That was one of the few times that my mother used the quick-cure method. Usually, if I've been a regular bum—not run errands or taken care of some other responsibility—she'll just nag me. It drives me crazy. Sometimes it seems as if I'll never hear the end of it, and at that point, I'll do anything she says.

My mother has been a big help to me this year. She helped me get a very good job helping out in an office a few blocks from here. I made one dollar and fifty cents an hour and I've been able to pay for my own books this year and to get a lot of clothes that I wanted. My mother's been working since I was about eleven, but something happened then that made it important for her to get out of the house. You see, I had a sister who was a few years older than me and she was terribly sick with leukemia. She died and it hit us all very hard, especially seeing her so weak, like she was the last year. My mother was terribly upset and going to work was a good way of getting her mind off my sister. She has an excellent job, however. She works as an administrative assistant to the head of a big foundation and really enjoys her work and is very efficient.

With the money I make from that job and from delivering clothes for the dry cleaner when he is busy, I don't need to ask my family for an allowance. If I have some big expenses, like expensive textbooks or an expensive piece of clothing, my family helps me out. Otherwise I've been able to take on a large share of my expenses myself this year. I hope I can help out this way in college, too. My family can afford to put me through without too much trouble, but I think it would be nice if I could take on the luxuries and extras myself.

That's the way my brother operated and he has set me a good example. I miss my brother very badly—greatly—since he's gone out of town to work. I really do. He's always been very good to me. Even though he is nine years older than I am, he's always taken me out to the show and to ball games and helped me with my schoolwork. He talks to me and helps me with any problems I've ever had. He's always been great. I haven't seen him for a couple of months, not since we all met upstate at my sister's college when she graduated in the spring. Then he had to go right back to his job in the Midwest. He is doing very well there, but he doesn't like living in such a small place and so far from the family and all his friends here.

I think he's now investigating other jobs. My brother is very independent and able to look after his own affairs very well. I think his plan is to line up several interviews with a few good possibilities and then to quit his job out there. He has learned everything he can from that situation and has advanced as far as that company will let him.

I really do hope it works out. I'd love to see him back here in New York.

# Neighborhood

The area in which these boys live contains
some of the most beautiful streets in New
York and also some of the ugliest. It has
a large park, playgrounds and ball fields,
a library, a museum, and a narcotics-addiction
center. Houses scattered throughout the
neighborhood are, from time to time, "raided
for dope" or for prostitution. These raids
take place around the corner from the many
well-kept and sometimes expensive apartment
houses of the area. The crime rate here is
relatively low for this borough of New
York City, although burglaries, muggings,
and juvenile complaints have vastly increased
over the neighborhood's own formerly low
rate. About 30 per cent of the population
is classified as "nonwhite."

Juan lives in a New York Housing
Authority Low Income Project, which faces
on a particularly unattractive commercial
area. More than nineteen hundred families
live in the nine buildings that comprise the
project. To qualify for residence, a family
with two children can earn no more than
$5,080 a year. Family income is closely
checked by Housing Authority employees,
who also may inspect individual apartments
at will to ascertain that building rules are
being complied with.

The area formerly contained small "old law
tenements" and "single-room occupancy"
dwellings that were condemned for bad
repair, dirt, disease, and crime. Juan lived
in one of these houses until it was demolished,

moved to another neighborhood for a few years, and returned when the project was completed.

Peter lives in a well-kept apartment house that was built on a fairly luxurious scale in the nineteen twenties. The building is on one of the nicer streets of the neighborhood, overlooking a large park. One hundred families live in the house. A doorman is always in attendance in the front lobby and the whole atmosphere seems remarkably friendly and intimate.

# Juan Gonzales

Man, I hate where I live, the projects. I've been living in a project for the past few years and I can't stand it. First of all, no pets. I've been offered so many times dogs and cats and I can't have them because of the Housing. Then there's a watch out for the walls. Don't staple anything to the walls because then you have to pay for it. Don't hang a picture. There's a fine. And they come and they check to make sure.

Don't make too much noise. The people upstairs and the people downstairs and the people on the side of you can hear every word and they've got to get some sleep. In the project grounds you can't play ball. In the project grounds you can't stay out late. About ten o'clock they tell you to go in or to get out. Then . . . there's trouble because they don't want you to hang around in the lobby. They're right about that one thing, because like in good houses, the lobby should be sort of like a show place, I think. You know, then you could have something special.

The elevators smell and they always break and you see even very old people tracking up and down the stairs. That's when the worst thing comes. People are grabbed on the stairs and held up or raped. There was this girl on the seventh floor who was raped and there was a girl on the fourth who was raped and robbed. There was an old man who was hit over the head— about fifty years old—he was hit over the head on the stairs and beat up bad. I don't know, maybe it's not always the people who live there. Maybe there's a party going on in the next-door and there are strangers in the party. You know how it is, not everybody is a relative. And those people come out and they start fights and arguments. Or they go around banging on the doors when they are drunk.

Before, when things happened in the halls, nobody would come out for nothing. When there were muggings, nobody wanted to come out in the halls and maybe have to face a guy with a knife or a gun. Lately, though, it's a little bit more friendly. Like my mother might have somebody come into our house to learn how to make rice and beans and then I tell my mother to go with them and learn how to make some American foods for a change. So now people are beginning to see on our floor that it's better to have someone help you if you are in trouble than to be alone and face the guy.

I guess in some ways the projects are better. Like when we used to live here before the projects, there were rats and holes and the building was falling apart. It was condemned so many times and so many times the landlords fought and won. The building wasn't torn down until finally it was the last building standing. And you know what that is, the last building . . . there's no place for those rats to go, or those bugs, or no place for the bums to sleep at night except in the one building still standing. It was terrible. The junkies and the drunks would all sleep in the halls at night and my mother was real scared. That was the same time she was out of work and it didn't look to us like anything was ever going to get better.

Then they were going to tear the house down. When I was about eleven or so we moved to another neighborhood. Down there I met one of the leaders of a gang called the Athletes, and the funny thing is that even though this boy was the leader, he didn't really want to belong to a gang. He only went into it because he was alone and everybody else was belonging. What could he do? Then I got associated with him and he quit his gang and we walked along together. Finally we had a whole group of us that were on our own. We still know each other. Even now sometimes I go over there or sometimes he comes here. When I was living there, sometimes he'd go away to Puerto Rico and I was always waiting for him to come back. You know, I missed him and he missed me.

My friend kept me from that fighting gang even though he was the leader. And he lived there with us, so we didn't have any trouble on the block because other gangs were afraid to come. We all lived together—Negroes, Puerto Ricans, and Italian kids—and we got along happy before I moved.

But my mother was afraid because the gang wars near the block made the other streets dangerous. You'd have all kinds of war. The Athletes would fight the Hairies. Then the newspaper had it the Hairies were fighting somebody else. My mother wanted to transfer back here, to the old neighborhood we'd lived in before the projects came.

Well, we did. But you know, every time you move you feel like it's not right because you're leaving part of yourself back there. I used to go back down there every weekend because, when we moved back here, everything was different. The projects were up, no more small houses, all twenty-one floors. There were new kids, a new school.

That time, before I knew anyone here on the block, I would have to fight a person to get introduced, and then finally either he'd beat me or I'd beat him. That way we'd get to know each other. I was new, you know. It was my building and my neighborhood, but I was new.

I would fight one guy in front of about twenty kids and I was afraid they were going to jump me. One time I said, "Look out, one guy and all of you gonna jump me. Is that a way to fight?" The guy I was fighting said they wouldn't jump me, and we fought that day and I went home bleeding. And then the next day I didn't get anybody to help me, but I went back and we fought again, and he beat me again. Then one day, I beat him. I proved him that I had courage and that I could succeed, and then, when the other boys came, this boy I had beaten up told them to lay off me.

Like back then, when I first came back to the neighborhood, my mother didn't want me to go out with all those kids on the street. I'd say to her, "Man, what am I going to do? I don't have any friends here. All I can do is just go out and look at people. You could go crazy." There were like groups of boys around and they stuck together. There were coloreds, Puerto Ricans, and Italian boys all together. But they were all friends with each other and they didn't want anybody crashing in on them. But after those fights we shook, and that was it. From then on, I was in.

In that gang the kids felt like they had protection, but now I think that it's better fighting for yourself. Otherwise you need the gang like an addict who needs the drug. You never see one of those boys fight anybody alone. Like in the school I used to go to, the junior high. They used to have lots of gangs there and it was rough in the nighttime or even in the daytime.

But whenever you'd meet one of those boys alone, you'd have no trouble with him. So what happens when they have nobody, when all their friends are in jail or when everybody else is killed, or something? What do they do?

They were chicken when they were alone and they couldn't think for themself. I wasn't used to that. With me, from the time I was eight, nine, ten, I was always on my own. Always running outside, figuring things out. I think I developed too young. I really did. My mind developed too quick, I think. I was thinking like an adult before I knew what was going on. I don't even think I liked being developed so young.

Of course, you get things in there if you do join a gang. First of all, you won't be bothered by this gang that you're joining. That's one. Second of all, you have protection. And three, you belong. You know that always comes up. You belong. You know, maybe your mother and father don't care, but one of these boys, if you plan to run away or something, they'll give you money or they'll keep you in their house for a while. You develop a friendship like brothers. Then, if you both think evil, that's what you do. You either run away together or do something that's against the law together or if you get caught, you get caught together. No one's going to run away from his buddy and leave him there with the cops. He'll either come back and hit the cop over the head, or he'll surrender.

But I got tired of it. You see, a while before they threw me out of the block, out of the club, all the little kids were smoking pot. Little guys, eight and nine years old. Well, that got me, and then, one day, I saw that there were boys sitting out there by the baker passing things back and forth. Little kids would come and pay them money and they would get pot. I didn't want that. I never took pot. I didn't want my little brother to do it or those little kids there either.

Like when I go to my school there are a lot of boys who do it, a lot of boys from my neighborhood who are in the school. I figure out that maybe those boys in my school who lived on my block were buying from the boys in the school and selling it home. Of course, I couldn't prove anything, but all I knew was that all of a sudden the little kids on the block were having it. So I figured out for myself that there's a time to tell and a time to keep quiet, and I figured that my time to tell had come. Or else I'd see my own little brother walking around with pot. So I told the policeman, but I told him not to tell my name. They got those boys and some of them they sent away and some of them they didn't.

Well, for a couple of days I didn't see anybody around the block and I decided not to hang around any more because I knew that I was going to get into trouble. But one day, I stayed in the movies too late, and I didn't get home until nine or nine thirty. It was very dark and there was nobody on the street, and as I walked along I saw them, all ganged up, about twenty-five of them, waiting. It was just like one of those things you see in the movies.

I figured they were going to kill me. I mean that's the first thing that comes into your mind. So I tried to bluff my way out. I didn't act scared. There they were, all lined up there on the stoop and I told them, "All right, I don't want any part of you." Right then and there I told them I didn't want anything to do with them and that there was going to be trouble for them because whatever I found out bad about them I was going to tell. I still know them, but I don't speak to them. Ever since that night they tried to jump me I consider them invisible. And somebody I consider invisible, I don't speak to, I say to myself, "They're not there." And I walk by.

Now, I've got my own one or two friends or I walk alone. I'm older, I don't care.

Things have cooled down in my neighborhood a lot. Old ladies, baby kids, all that kind walking around, playing. There's not much to do, so what we sometimes do is we look for a place. We look for something you can do that's exciting, that's fun. We go out to have fun, some excitement in there. It doesn't have to be exactly fighting, but lots of times there's a fight on Friday nights around my block. At the playground, or in the park. You find out about it like you know when there's going to be dances, or when there's going to be a little club meeting. The same way, I know usually when there's going to be a fight.

Maybe I see somebody and he says, "Hey, man, come to the playground or come up to the park and we're going to have a fight at seven thirty. Bring a knife, you know, or a club or something." And you go up and twenty or thirty guys go up there and fight for half an hour or an hour. Usually they have two or three young ones looking out for the police.

Lots of times the young kids in the group, just starting out, they get the worst of the beating. Because that kind of kid, he's stupid. I mean, everybody else is way over his age, but he wants to prove he's a big man. So he gets beat up two or three times, or else he's the one that might kill a guy because he can't fight him with fists, so he has to fight him with a knife or something.

Usually everybody is carrying a knife, but nobody much uses it. Only if three or four guys are jumping on one boy, and there's only that one way out. Everybody tries to start with a fist fight, though.

But there's one thing I don't ever do. I don't ever fight with my friends, even if they're on the other side. It's better to hit somebody you don't know than hit one of your own friends.

Usually the police get in the way. We've been caught a couple of times, but we make believe we're just sitting and watching, and you say, "Well, I had nothing to do with this, officer," and most of the time you get away with it.

Around my block, there aren't too many of these fights, only once every two or three weeks. But where my friend lives, over in Jersey, it happens every Friday. Over there, they seem to fight more often. Over there the police are worse; different, way different. They insult the people, they have a curfew. Every policeman has a J.D. card on everybody in the neighhood, everybody that's walking on the street. And the police there have no kind of decency. They stop girls and take them home and assault them themselves. And the girls can't say anything about them because it's their word against his. And the boys get beat up for no reason, like Jack, my friend, and his friends are always being beat up like that.

Sometimes you go to the fight for the excitement, or because you don't want to be called chicken, or just to see what's going on around the block. But usually you have to get into it because, you know, they say, "What are you looking at?"

Once a boy got caught up on the barbed-wire fence. He was

cut up, stuck up there with his chest caught and everything. And there was only one thing to do—run. The police were right behind us, and anyway we couldn't do anything for that boy. What were we going to do? Take him to the hospital? And then the police would ask what happened to him? So when the police were coming, we all ran. When they got that boy down off the fence, he was pretty close to dying. His chest was all cut up and he'll always have a lot of scars from that. Well, his parents had him put away in a home. I guess that's better than letting him stay around here and get himself killed.

But that kid, he was crazy. I mean, only a little boy, fourteen or fifteen, and he started fighting with those big guys.

It's funny. I can't really explain what a real tough guy is. My little brother says that a guy that never talks, and walks alone, is a tough guy. But then, there's the other tough guy who has a gang that's strong. Or a Puerto Rican kid, who's maybe built up his physique. He's tough, I guess, but not the Paddy boy who took a few boxing lessons. He's not tough. Those kids in Jersey are supposed to be real tough, there's so many gangs there. But once I went there with my friend and we were walking down the street. There were three boys ahead of us and they were about the same age and the same size as we are. And two of them were Puerto Ricans and one was colored. They started laughing at one of us, I don't know which. Since I figured it was me, I stepped right on that guy's foot, and I kept my foot there, and I walked right across him. Well, we were walking ahead now, and I wondered what was going to happen. But they were all quiet and still. I turned right around to my friend and I said, "These are your big gangster friends? They just chicken out."

Friday night is supposed to be the night everybody in town fights down there, but we couldn't find anything. I was looking for a fight because this was supposed to be a tough neighborhood, and it gets me mad because they have this big reputation and they were all hanging around big and tough, but you insult them, you step on them, and they won't do anything.

Around here, if I can't find a fight on my own block, I go to the East Side. Once, we ran into a gang there and by luck

I happened to say where I was from. They had a treaty with my neighborhood and it was all right, but if you make a simple mistake, like on a train, and you land up in Brooklyn, it's a big difference. You say you're from my neighborhood—well, they might kill you. If I got off the subway, and let's say I was trying to round up boys for a fight of ours, Brooklyn wouldn't be the place to go.

It's kind of impossible to have a treaty with one of the gangs over there. The War Lords don't know each other and they don't know the same enemies. The only time you could really have a treaty where all four or five boroughs get together would be if the adults were going to attack us, you know, and everybody would have to get together. It would have to be something really big like that. Usually, Brooklyn doesn't want any New York boys coming over there and asking for help and he doesn't want New York boys coming over there and walking on their territory.

It works out simple. Let's say that I am the leader of one of the gangs and three or four guys come over to me and start beating me up and I know they're not from this neighborhood. This doesn't go. I mean, I can't go over there and start fighting those guys myself. So what I do is, I contact all the boys all over the place that I know, or that we have treaties with. And I get them all out. You have to have a lot to go over to the East Side. I tell them to go in small groups, here and there, and to meet on the East Side in a special place.

All of us go over there and I go to the leaders on the other side and I say that four boys jumped me last week and I want to see his gang and to have them stand up so I can find out if any of those were in their gang. And the leader goes and does it or else we have an all-out war.

But there is not too much fighting now. Down further on the street they were really a fighting gang. They used to run around in cars with all their equipment—knives, guns, grenades—in the back. Then they just got tired of cutting all those little guys, so they moved. They got old and decided to settle down to a peaceful life, raising up their hoodlum children.

I suppose the little kids are still doing all that, but, anyhow, gangs change their name every day because they don't want the police chasing them and it's hard to keep track. If you're a Persian Angel, man, and somebody in your group kills somebody, you change your name real quick.

Another thing is, white kids don't belong to gangs much. They're usually cowards. Only maybe sometimes, if one white, he lived around a colored neighborhood for a long time, and he proved he's not scared, then they take him in. Me, I'm not afraid of tough kids. It's bad when you're afraid of them. Like a Paddy boy will chicken out if he was alone. Really scared to death, you know. But not me. Oh, I was smeared a lot of times—smeared is you don't have a chance. I was jumped in the park a couple of times. I was jumped down there once by a group of guys I didn't even know. Those guys jumped on me and started beating the heck out of me, kicking, cursing, using their cigarettes. That time I went to the hospital and they patched me up and took me home. But the thing is I wasn't afraid of them. Why they did so good, what happened, was they just caught me by surprise. I mean I would have caught a couple of them and they wouldn't have been able to hurt me that badly, but the trouble was they caught me by surprise and I didn't have a chance. If I knew them I would kill them afterwards. Do you think I would come home bandaged up, and you think I'm not going to do anything about it? I get riled sometimes when a guy looks at me the wrong way. You think I'm not going to get those that got me? I'll get them one at a time if I'm alone, or all at once if I have a group with me. I'm not scared to walk down the street ever. I can handle myself and I might take on a guy, he's alone, because I've seen him act big when he's with his men and now I want to test him, like alone. But taking on a whole gang, that's another thing.

Going home from school once, there was big trouble like that. On the subway, right on the train when it was moving, some guys grabbed a couple of white school girls . . . and they raped them. I couldn't stand it, right there on the subway and they did it without interference. That's something in my life I'm not proud of.

Man, you believe me? I ran all over that train trying to find a cop. And I wouldn't have minded jumping in and stopping it, no matter what, if there was a way. I got very upset but, see, I go in there, without a knife, alone, I'm going to get my brains knocked out. Even that, I wouldn't mind so bad, if I knew the girls were going to come out all right. But I knew they were still going to be played around with.

And there was nobody else who wanted to come with me. I don't think the guys I was with, they cared at all. Nobody would help me, not old people or kids. On that whole train, nobody, nobody. I was alone.

I feel lousy about it. I mean, even now, sometimes I look at a girl and I think, "Suppose that happened again? What would I do *this* time?" And I promise myself I'll go in, no matter what. But I couldn't do anything about it that time. I'm not afraid to fight, I've been fighting all my life. But nobody would help me start a little riot and get them off those girls.

There are some times, though, when everybody in the neighborhood does get together, agrees on one thing. Like the time there was one policeman who used to tease and bother everybody around the block. It got so bad that we had to fix that policeman. So everybody got together. Nobody was on the street that day except one boy, up on a stoop. The policeman said, "Get off. Get off that stoop. You don't belong here." Well, the boy stepped quickly back and the cop came up on the stoop. Up above there on the roof, they had a garbage can and they sent it right on his head. He was in the hospital for about three or four months, something wrong with his head. And the next policeman they sent wasn't so bad; he was just bad like a regular policeman.

The police are the most crooked, the most evil. I've never seen a policeman that was fair or that was even good. All the policemen I've ever known are hanging around in the liquor store or taking money from Jim on the corner, or in the store on the avenue. They're just out to make a buck no matter how they can do it. O.K., maybe if you gave them more money they wouldn't be so crooked, but what do you need to qualify for a policeman? I mean, if you have an ounce of brain and you have sturdy shoulders and you're about six feet one, you can be a policeman. That's all.

I mean, you've got to fight them all the time. A policeman is supposed to be somebody that protects people. You're supposed to be able to count on them. You're supposed to look up to policemen and know that if anything goes wrong, if any boys jumped me, I can just yell and the policeman will come running and save me. Around my block, you get jumped, the police will say, "Well, that's just too bad." He just sits there.

Even the sergeants are crooked. It's the whole police force is rotten. There was a man, I don't know who he was, way out in Brooklyn somewhere. He broke down a whole police station, a whole police force, the detectives, the policemen, the rookies. Everybody that was on that police force was crooked. Everybody in the precinct was crooked. He had to tell them all to go home.

Like take the Negro cop. The police towards discrimination are the same as anybody else. You have colored policemen, Italian policemen, every kind. But, you know, a Negro policeman will tend to beat up another Negro more than he would beat up anybody else, because he says to himself, "I'm a cop, and this guy is going to expect special privileges. I've got to show the other people it doesn't mean anything to me, that I'm really not going to treat them different." I think the Puerto Ricans would be just the same as the Negroes. He would tend to beat up Puerto Rican people more than he would a Negro or anybody else. Maybe you think he'd feel the Puerto Ricans were somebody he should help and he should try to solve some of their problems. But that's not the way it works.

And like I said, you think they protect you? When I lived downtown, it was a terrible neighborhood. There were so many killings, and people were being raped and murdered and all. Guys, you could see them, guys you could see jumping out of windows, running away from a robber, using a needle or something. I worked in a grocery there and I was afraid to go to work, but I guess I was lucky anyhow. I mean, I never got in any kind of real cop trouble or anything. They'd pick me up only in sort of like routine. They picked up everybody once in a while to make sure, you know, that nobody is carrying weapons and there is not going to be a fight that day. Of course, as soon as the police left, everything was the same all over again, anyhow.

That time they picked me up, I was halfway home from the grocery store where I worked and—well—I'll tell you how I felt like. I felt like the policeman was the rottenest person in the world. What would happen, see, is that I was always tall, and being tall, they think that I'm older. Then, no matter what you tell them, they believe that you're older. They were looking for a draft card and I didn't have one. I was too young and I told them I didn't have a draft card. Man, I was only twelve, thirteen or so, you know. Then they'd take me on the side and hit me a couple of times and I'd go home black and blue.

You wouldn't get picked up alone, even now. A person alone they never bother with, unless he's looking at cars or something. Whenever I get picked up, it's with a group. Like if I'm walking along and there's a group here and at the same time I'm walking, even though I don't know them, a policeman comes. They take all of us. Once I got picked up when there was a poker game going on or a crap game. They picked us up and they wanted to find out who had the money, who had the dice. They hit everybody. I think I even got hit the worst because I was a little taller than the rest of them. It happens right out on the street.

They tell you to get up against the wall of a building, and then they start searching you. And you can't talk to the policeman. Never say a word when they have you against the wall. Say anything and he thinks that you are making a false move and then he has the right to shoot you. So I would stand there and he asked my name, and I'd tell. And then he'd ask for my age and when I'd tell him twelve, thirteen, fourteen, he wouldn't believe me. They didn't think a Puerto Rican kid could be so young, so tall. Then they'd take me over the side and hit me a couple of times.

I'd be scared. Half the time I was petrified from being hit and because I was thinking of what my mother would say, you know, if I was taken down to the station. That I didn't do anything didn't make any difference to the police because

I was still picked up. But I guess I was lucky because every time I was picked up I got sent home. There were a couple of boys that time that were Spanish and they didn't understand the language too well. When they tried to tell the policeman something, they got black and blue marks all over. Well, they didn't like it too much and they started trying to run away and talking back and pushing around, you know. The policeman just grabbed them, got them in the car and took them away. But me, I never went to the station house.

It's happened twice over here, too. See, when I was still hanging around the block, when we first came here, I used to go up the street. But twice I got picked up there. Once, this boy asked me for a light up there on the corner. He was with some friends, so I gave it to him. I didn't want to start any trouble. Just then the police came.

First of all, they didn't like smoking. They took the cigarettes and tore them up. Second, they didn't like the way the boys were hanging around the corner. They thought they were insulting the people walking by. You know, when a person is walking by and there's a bunch of boys, they maybe start looking at people as if they were trash, or start calling names, or if they see a girl walking by, they call her a name or grab something up. So, me, I agreed with the policeman that time, but he sure didn't agree with me.

Well, that time the cops started searching. Now I don't like being searched and as I get older I'm—I'm sort of ready to strike out. Well, they searched us and one of the boys had a knife. It was John, and he was about seventeen then. By the way, his father was the one who was killed in that bar—he was working in a bar and a man shot him? Well, anyway, John had a knife that he used just for fooling around with a piece of wood or for fishing sometime. John isn't the kind of guy that would ever use a knife. The policeman took it and asked him what he was going to do with it and John told him that it was his fishing knife. The policeman said, "You're not fishing now." The cop hit him and he hit me. He hit me because I was taller than he was and he'd asked again for the draft card. Now, I get very mad when they ask me for that. And John was crying and I was on the verge of tears, you know, because the night stick really hurts. But they let us go after that. There was a whole crowd there and I felt very embarrassed, you know. People watching you and girls, and old people that know your family and they see you being picked up.

Then there was another time. I wasn't even there, but there were a bunch of boys and a couple of girls all standing out in the hall that sort of extends into the stoop. They were playing cards, poker for pennies and nickels—nothing more. Well, an old lady came walking by, and she couldn't get past in the hall, and they were bothering her, sort of. She went up and called the police and just as the police car was coming down the block, I was walking down the street. At the same time that I hit that stoop, walking by that stoop, they came out of the car and grabbed all of us. They took us and they lined us up. They took the other kids' money, but I was broke that day, so I felt good. At least, you know, they didn't get anything from me that time.

The way it goes, other times, if you're playing cards, the police say that the money you've got in your pockets is from playing and they take all of it. That time they lined us up and asked our age and boy, I was the oldest one. I told them that I was just walking by, and they said, "Oh, yeah. We know." And I got the worst of it. They took down my name and they gave me a J.D. card. A juvenile delinquent! That's a good one for you. Me, after all this, I'm suddenly a juvenile. Then, if that wasn't bad enough, they wanted to take me home. Can you imagine being driven home? And then they leave you right in front of the door and you get out of a police car where you live. That's the worst thing. That police car right in front of the building with my mother living there and all.

I've always lived in this neighborhood. My parents moved to a house up the street a few years after they got married and they lived there until we moved to this building about eleven years ago. We've lived in this same building ever since, and my aunt and uncle and cousins have lived here even longer. My grandfather still lives a few blocks away, so we Quinns really are settled in here.

The apartment house we live in has run down lately like other parts of the neighborhood. My family is afraid it's going to turn into a high-class slum. There is always something being repaired with the plumbing or the electricity, since the building is pretty old now. You have to wait a longer time to get some repairs done and my mother says the service is not nearly as good as it used to be. For example, there was always a doorman at each entrance all day and all night. Now they've taken off the doorman at the back door for a few hours during the night. Another problem is that the elevators are now self-service and it's not nearly as convenient as it used to be, when there were elevator men.

We're lucky though. There's a very funny man in the house who really does a good job about all these complaints. He organizes meetings, and gets the lawyers who live here to advise him, and the tenants to pay a yearly fee for his committee, and I don't know what else. He's really a scream. I *love* him. I think he's great when meetings are held, and he really does accomplish things. The landlord has learned by now that he can't get away with anything because we're always alert to our rights.

I don't have any complaints about our own apartment though. It's spacious and has a great view of the park and my mother and sister are really great at interior decorating. I have my own room now. I used to share it with my brother, but since he's away it's exclusively for me. His bed is still there, though, and I wouldn't be sorry to have him back using it.

Aside from my sister's room and my parent's bedroom, there's a living room, dining room, kitchen and three bathrooms. My own room is really neat, the best room I know of in the world. It's got dark brown walls and orange bedspreads. I've got a guitar on the wall, a wine bottle, my school athletic letter. I love to hang things on the wall. There are two bachelor chests in the room, one for my brother, one for myself, bookcases, and trophies on a shelf, and my own desk. My brother and I each have our own closet and we fitted them very nicely with places for shoes and athletic equipment. Then there's a great big comfortable chair in my room which is the best thing to get into when you want to be off by yourself.

Sometimes, of course, my family thinks about moving because the neighborhood, in the side streets, and over in the projects, isn't what it used to be. You hear about people being mugged now and problems with gangs and all the rest.

When I was small, I knew everybody around our street; everybody was my friend. Every day all the kids would meet out at the park—we used to call it the big park. And every day we played skully bones with bottle tops and games like that and maybe threw a ball a little bit. I had no worries then. That is, I've never fought between my own friends and there weren't so many Puerto Rican or colored kids around. Now, sometimes, when I leave the house at night or have to meet off in the park somewhere, I am afraid. Or when I walk down the street and I see four Puerto Ricans—and I could tell them a mile away, not that they're Puerto Rican, but that they're that type that looks like they're going to kill anybody that steps in front of them—I am really terrified. I steer clear, I cross the street.

My friends never, never look for trouble. We don't like it. If we're coming head on to one of those gangs, we cross. I'll give them the right of way anytime if they think that makes them big. There've been a few incidents like that where these guys think that by being tough they really are getting something when it's really a laugh. Once, when I was a lot younger, a colored kid stopped me and asked me if I had any money on me. I told him I had two cents and I said,

"You want it?" He answered that he did want it and that he would buy some lunch with it. I said, "Go ahead, buy all the lunch you can get with that."

Of course, not all Puerto Rican kids are like that or all colored, I guess. One guy, Fernando Gutierrez, is in our group and even he once got into trouble with them. One day we were all playing ball in the big park and he had a beautiful glove that cost his father about twenty dollars. A bunch of Puerto Rican and colored kids came out and they grabbed his glove and told him that they wouldn't give it back unless we gave them some money. Well, we chipped in and we got about fifty cents together and they sold the glove back to us for the fifty cents. They didn't even know what it was worth.

The trouble is that, living as they do, there wouldn't be much else for them to look forward to besides picking up a name for being tough. All they're looking for is a reputation, since they don't have much else to look for. I saw on a TV show once a story about a Puerto Rican boy who was really typical. That boy said that during the school year the one thing he looked forward to was lunch in the school cafeteria because it was the biggest meal he had. He kind of liked school because there isn't much for him to do otherwise except sit outside on the stoop.

Of course, they're not all like that. Two Puerto Rican boys who are with our group from our church—well, they're on our side. Because they've always gone where we've gone, they know how we think and what we like to do, and that we don't like to fight. They both go to good schools and don't have anything to do with the others. When . . . if ever there is an emergency, they're with us.

The one time we've had serious problems with those gangs was a few months ago. A group of us, about fifteen, had been up at a private pool swimming and when we came out, we were standing around saying good night. One real big kid, a friend of mine, had a soda which he was drinking and a bunch of Puerto Rican kids came along. They asked him to give them a drink out of his bottle and he wouldn't. He said that he'd just bought it and that everybody was taking a sip and that he wouldn't have anything left for himself. Well, one thing led to another, but my friend wasn't going to stand for being pushed around. He said, "I'm not going to let anyone push me or my friends around." Well, that did it. They left, but the next day the same boys came up to us, this time when we were standing in front of the gym. They gave us an ultimatum. They said that they would give us three choices: either we fight them; we back down; or we never go over onto their block. They left then and we were very worried.

Of course, there's quite a large group of us, too, who go to church, club meetings and play ball together and maybe go to dances together or date. But we are not any kind of fighting group. Nobody among us likes to fight, and we'll do anything we can to stop one. That time, it was a Saturday, and we went down to the gym in the cellar of the church and we set up chairs for the next morning's Mass. All the fellows got together there and we had a democratic meeting and a few suggestions were made. We decided that if we ever fought those boys everyone of us would be killed, really. Those Puerto Rican and colored kids from the projects can get so many others of their own kind in such a short time, it's really unbelievable. They get them from all over the city within a few hours by telephone, telling what's going on. It's sort of a chain. They're called War Lords or something like that, and they even have treaties.

We knew that, once we set up a fight, perhaps three or four hundred of them would show up. Another thing is, they'd all be armed. They have knives and chains and probably even pistols. I've never seen a Puerto Rican or a colored kid use a weapon on a white boy, though I've heard of it. What I did see was one Puerto Rican kid beat another one with a chain. That's a vicious weapon.

Well, we talked about how the incident had started, how we might have avoided it, what was going to happen that night, what the odds would be. We worked it out that it was fifteen to one against us, at the very least. The solution seemed simple. We decided to back down by saying, as we backed down, that we would not go as a group into their block. We met with one or two of them and we told them that when we saw them in a gang, on the street, we wouldn't say anything, wouldn't look at them. We would just ignore them as they would ignore us. That night, a meeting was arranged, with all of us on one side of the street and all of them on the other. One of our boys went out into the middle of the street. He says he felt very frightened and could see that they had weapons with them. Well, the two leaders met in the middle and discussed the matter and it all broke up. My friend was a fast talker and got us out of this by brains and not by muscle.

The thing is that we don't have to look for reputations, we don't have to pick up a name for being good fighters. We had decided all that in our strategic meeting and we all knew that it was a stupid move to fight. All we did was to provide those fools with another notch to their guns without losing anything ourselves. When you're dealing with that type, there's nothing to be ashamed of for having more brains. I'm not sure how to say it, but I think they felt a little bigger by showing us that they could put us down, because that's how they interpreted it.

The truth of the matter is that they don't like us and we don't like them. We come from Holy Family and we're white. They either don't go to church at all or go to the other parish, and they're colored—or Puerto Rican. According to their rules, making whites ashamed, as they thought they did, was real important. Then, the next time, when they see us using the private pool, or going off to the club to play ball, or driving by in our parents' car, they could feel that they were superior. The truth is that we were smart enough not to lose our heads.

There were two policemen around that night, but they didn't do anything. The policemen just told us to walk around and go home, but they didn't interfere because there was nothing really happening. The police do step in when there's any trouble, though. For example, there's one boy who lives in the project, but he hangs around most of the time with us. One night he was cutting across the playground of the project and a bunch of kids jumped him and were beating him up pretty badly. The police came along at just the right moment and got all those kids.

In general, the police in New York do a very good job. I

think all this fuss about police discrimination and so forth is not true. Perhaps, once in a while, you can get a policeman who will be too rough or dishonest, but it's that way in any large group. Another problem is that if I were a policeman and I were offered $100,000 to forget about a gambling syndicate or something like that, I'd find it very hard to refuse. And I know there must be some policemen who are weaker than I am. Even with traffic violations, if they don't jeopardize anyone's life, I think it must be very hard to resist if someone gives you some money. It doesn't matter that much.

The police are just trying to do their job and if you know your rights, you're all right. For example, a bunch of us often meet up at the luncheonette at the corner and have Cokes in the evening when there's no school. Well, the proprietor doesn't like one of my friends and one night he just pushed him out. He was buddies with the policeman on the beat and he called him. When the policeman put his hand on my friend, my friend really began shouting. He told him, "I know just who you are and what you can do to me and what you can't. If you touch me again, my father will bring suit against the whole city government. I will not be discriminated against." Well, my friend was making such a fuss and drawing such a crowd, the policeman just slunk away and we went back to drinking our Cokes.

Another time something like that happened to my best friend. He goes to Europe with his family every summer, and last year he brought back a BB gun. We went into the park to a secluded place and he was trying out his gun on some pigeons—not that he could hit them, anyhow. Well, someone must have seen us and reported us to the police. The police came into the park and as soon as my friend saw them he put the gun into his pocket. The police shouted "Stop," but when John turned around and saw them he got scared and he began to run. He ran for many blocks until finally there was a policeman in front of him and policemen on both sides and they all had their guns drawn. They shouted, "Stop, or we'll shoot." Well, John stopped and fell to the ground so he wouldn't get hit and they put handcuffs on him and took him to the police station.

By the time I saw him next day there wasn't a clean place on him. He was black and blue all over, both arms were bruised, and he was really in bad shape.

I know he shouldn't have run, but he didn't want to get caught. He knew that police regularly beat people and I know for myself that I wouldn't want to be picked up by a policeman either. If I thought I had done something wrong, I would run away as far as I could.

Well, my friend's father was out of town on business, but his mother went down to the precinct as soon as she heard. The police told her that luckily all this had taken place during the day because otherwise he might have been really hurt. They said that the ballistics report showed that the gun had only been used for BB's and so he was safe. Well, when my friend's mother saw the condition he was in, she was very angry and I think she threatened to sue. But nothing ever came of it that I heard.

The police took his gun, I guess took it home for their own kids. But, really, it was a good job they did. They didn't know what he was doing with that gun and it taught him a lesson. I'm on the law's side. After all, he could have seriously hurt somebody with those BB's which are very powerful. This way, he really learned his lesson.

In a way, it's funny that this particular boy was the one who got into trouble. He's really very smart and has very strong opinions about everything. He won a medal for the German language and I consider him one of my intellectual friends. You know, out of a large group, there are a few who are more serious-minded and perhaps who use a better vocabulary and that sort of thing.

Actually, most of my friends, my really close ones, come from the neighborhood. I know some boys at school very well, but it's not the same. Most of the kids I still see are the kids I graduated from Holy Family with. They're from this immediate area, and even though most of them are in different schools now, we still see each other. I guess you could say I belong to sort of a clique. You know, kids say, "You in a clique?" And then they make this funny clicking noise, just for a joke, you know. There must be about thirty boys in all, though we don't see each other most of the time in big groups and only about ten or twelve are really close to me. Once we thought we'd try to get a club together from out of this group and get a clubhouse, too. There was an empty store up on the street that was just right around the corner from the church. It was a very convenient meeting place and we were trying to get it under the Church's name, under the supervision of some priest or of the Church itself.

Well we had the approval of the Church and we had everything set. But then we were advised by one of the younger priests and by a social worker who was a very good friend of ours that, once we have a group in a room where you've got pool tables or dart boards and a Coke machine, you have troubles. He said then all those other people, people from all over whom we've only seen once or twice, are going to come and want to be taken in. He said we'd have a fight on our hands every night and never have any privacy, so we gave the whole idea up.

Generally I speak to my friends at least once a day, either by phone or when we meet up at the pool or at the gym. Usually when I get home from school I can't stand to look at my work. I'd keel over if I had to. I change my clothes and rush out to play ball or to circulate around the church with the other kids. If the weather's bad, we might play some games or talk.

We play ball a lot, stickball. This is a game I really love. It's great. Then, in season, we have our own football team, two squads on a football team. We don't play in a league, though; just play in the neighborhood. Once, just for fun, we patched together some old uniforms and bought letters that stood for the block we live on and some kids got some of those Confederate flags. We pasted all that on top of our helmets and got a lot of fun out of it.

Sometimes in the park when we're picking up a basketball game or maybe looking for a football team to play, we've played with strange kids and that's a good way to make friends. There was one time when we got into a terrible fight over it, but once in a while you make good friends that way, and get to know them better.

Most of the kids in our group come from about the same kind of families. Oh, there are different nationalities—some Irish, a couple of French, one German, a couple of Scots. But we are all about the same, from comfortable families. Of course, we are all saving for something. One guy is saving all his pennies to buy drums. That's all he wants now is drums. But lately, for most of us, it's been driving, that's the big thing. I mean that's natural. Either driving a car or even a motorcycle. One of my friends has a motorcycle and we get a big kick out of working on it. He let me ride it the other day and it was thrilling. You put your hands on the handle bars and go. I couldn't get up very fast, but it was really something. It's a completely different experience from anything else.

Now, I'm taking driving lessons, though my parents are a little worried about that. At first, we didn't tell my father that I have a permit, but then when I wanted to practice, we had to. My mother is the most worried. She'll say things like, "I'm one hundred per cent for your driving, but I don't want you to drive." Stuff like that you know that just turns you, running around in a circle. Circular reasoning.

I think it's a real privilege to drive. I'm dying for a car of my own. A few weeks ago one of the priests in the parish, who often drives us out to the beach, asked us if we would like to take the car out for a little drive. We promised we'd take good care of it and we went out and had a great time in it. When we brought the car back, we put a full tank of gas in and left it in front of the rectory door.

I should be saving up for a car, or at least to help buy one, but that's the trouble. I save and save and then one day I will be walking down the street and I'll see a man in a blue blazer with silver buttons and a nice little crest, and I go crazy. I really want that blazer that day. But the next day I'll be walking along and I'll hear a big, powerful motorcycle. Or else another day I'll have to get a pair of skis or some great book bag. It's a real weakness of mine. A car would be great though, especially when the weather's good.

Summers have changed, now that I'm older. We used to go either to the Day Camp the club ran or else my mother would take us out to Voyer's Island, which is a resort the club runs.

We'd swim every day, play tennis, get a full day just like we were living at the beach. Then, we'd come home and have dinner, or sometimes, if my dad could make it, or he was away on business, we'd eat at the club.

Now I go to the beach with my friends a lot during the summer when we're not working at summer jobs or away with our families. We take the train, or get a ride with one of the adults. Then we all meet in one spot and spend the day.

Sometimes girls from our own group come with us or sometimes the boys just go by themselves. You might see a group of eight or ten girls down there whom you don't know and you might talk to them, but I've never dated one of those girls or really spent any time with them. You see, we know all the kids we need to. I never really had to make new friends because we never changed out of the neighborhood.

# Schools

Juan attended the local public elementary
school in first grade and then in fifth and
sixth grades, when his family moved back into
the neighborhood. This school is 90 per cent
"nonwhite." On the whole, middle-class
families, who can manage to, send their
children to private day schools, to parochial
schools, or to a few special tax-supported
schools where high grades or special talents are
required. This is true of the middle-class white
population and also of the few middle-class
Negro families in the neighborhood, though it
frequently entails burdensome financial
sacrifice.

After graduating from elementary school,
Juan went to the junior high school that
services his district and now attends a rather
distant vocational high school which happens
to give the automotive course he was advised
to take. The school had somewhat less than
two thousand students. An attempt is made
to keep academic classes at thirty-nine
members each, but there are, in fact,
between forty and fifty students in most of
these classes. Shop classes are smaller.

Peter now attends an academic Catholic
high school for boys which is run by an order
noted for its strict discipline. There are about
seven hundred students in the school and
most classes have about thirty students. Peter
came to this school from the neighborhood
parochial elementary school which he attended

from the time he was five. Although more Puerto Rican children are now registered there, when he attended, the student body was almost entirely white.

# Juan Gonzales

I don't think, if I have to live in this neighborhood when I get older, I would let my son go to P.S. 305* or 96** or any of the other schools that I went to. I would do something like the middle class does. I would get a tutor, one of the best, and let him teach my son or daughter everything he has to know.

My school is bad. I really think it was the only thing my parents could do to send me there and it has no problems for *me*, but it's bad all right.

You know, kids walk down the halls, just walking down. They bump into somebody, they slug somebody, a kid always feels like he is being pushed. The kids, especially in the Adjustment classes, the kids are rough. You know what Adjustment classes are? Oh, boy! The teacher, he sees you doing something wrong, he doesn't ask you, out you go to the office.

I didn't do anything to get there. I just transferred from P.S. 305 to the seventh grade in 96 and I had to go into an Adjustment class and *wham*! I was in that class and I knew I had to get out. I couldn't stand it. I asked for a transfer and they wouldn't give it to me, so what I did was that I studied real hard and my marks went up to 90-95. Study! All the time I studied to get out of there. My marks went up to 90-95 and the teacher said, "Well, this kid doesn't belong here. He sits in that little corner over there. He keeps quiet. He doesn't forget his work; he comes nicely prepared. How can you keep a boy here like that?"

So they took me out and put me in honor class. From then on I have been in an honor class. But, even so, what I'm saying is that I wouldn't let my kids go to a school like that.

Now you see, you take your boy and you bring him up not to curse, not to say bad words, not to do anything wrong, not to smoke pot, or drink, or anything. And then he goes to school and there are five hundred to a thousand boys there

* Elementary School
** Junior High School

and they are opposite him. All they *do* is curse. All they *do* is have bad manners. All they *do* is fight and make trouble for the boys. How are you going to keep your boy from turning out the same way? Like taking pot?

One thing, I never took pot. I wouldn't be standing here if I did. I'd turn myself in.

There used to be a lot of kids who took dope in school. They'd be passing it under the tables at the lunchroom and in the classroom. And then they would have it outside at three o'clock, or in the morning they would be out there, saying, "Seventy-five cents. You want one? Go on and try one." Lately, those types have been cooling down around us big guys in the school. The big guys, especially now, they don't come near us. They know it's bad, but they don't use it mostly because those who took it, they've dropped out now. The ones that are left, they don't want to take a chance. Nobody wants to be kicked out after all these years, just because they're carrying a stick, or tasting powder, or using it in a handkerchief.

The younger boys still do it because they don't know what they're up against. See, somebody tells them not to worry about getting the habit and they want to try the kicks out of it.

Like Silva, a friend of mine, real close. He used to take it when he was in his first year here. I was with him even then, and I asked him why he did it. He tells me and he tells me, and what he says is, "Well, I feel good, I feel good inside. After all the crap I feel good, I get away from it all with this stick. I feel strong, important. Sometimes I just feel—*myself*."

Me, I want to forget all about that now. Silva is off it now, too. We took each other in hand and he doesn't go around with that gang that smokes pot any more.

In my school there are mostly Puerto Ricans and Negroes, but in my honor classes, there are almost all whites. They're all trying for careers that you have to have a very good average for. They all want to go to college, so they have to have a good average. They get into the honor class very easily.

But there is no favoritism in our school. That's one thing I like about it. Everybody has to do their own work to get what they want. And there's really no trouble with the whites as long as they stay on their own side. You know, it's sort of like, "You leave me alone, I'll leave you alone."

There was only one tough guy in all the whites and I took him on. He was pushing everybody in the honor class around, picking on his own race, and then picking up on everybody else. I was second tallest, like now, and I wasn't afraid of that big mouth at all. I punched him in the face and I told him to sit down and to keep his mouth shut and not to bother anybody in the class. The teacher was right there when it happened, but he didn't say anything. There was nothing he could do about it and he was glad that I got that guy into line. I mean, everybody's sixteen, seventeen years old. The teacher's not going to come and stop one boy, because then he might have the whole class on him. So he lets us do what we want, but he writes it down. That time he didn't write anything down about me punching that kid because he was looking for somebody to take care of him, anyhow.

There isn't too much trouble these days in my classes. By the time you get to the junior or senior year, you can't afford to do anything you might get thrown out for. Before now, most kids were just staying in school because the law says they have to. They didn't think that it would matter later on, so they would insult the teacher and ask for a fight.

There once was a big fight in my math class in junior high. We were all playing around just waiting for the bell to ring but, like always, pretty soon it turned into a big fight, with four or five fights going on right there in the room. The teacher came and he tried to break them up; but some kid jumped him, too, and they beat him up bad.

He quit the school, teaching, everything. Funny thing, I saw him one day on the bus and he's a nice, young, clean-cut fellow, you know. And when I saw him that time, after he left, he looked so—you know—so nice, I was really sorry it happened.

But he could never handle the class. They were always throwing paper airplanes, cursing at him, and asking for fights all the time. So it was lucky for him to get out. Anyway he did better, got a better job.

With teachers, it all depends on how they handle themselves. They ought to make sure the kids don't think they are playing favoritism. They've got to be fair with all the boys so that it's all free. And if you have like a Negro little kid, and maybe a big white kid who is bothering him, the teacher's got to stop that. They can't tolerate that because they know that any little thing could start a racial riot.

But like I said, we don't have much race trouble in my school. We stay on our own sides. Like I never see the kids in the honor classes after school. After school, everybody leads their own lives. I don't go to their place and they don't come to mine. But with the Spanish boys, I know a lot of them and I go to their houses. We have a good time even though maybe they come from a different neighborhood, too. The Spanish boys go with the Spanish boys, the white boys go with the white.

But it doesn't really make a difference in the colors when you go to school. The trouble is, how could I go to a colored's house when he didn't want to be ashamed because he lived in a bad place, or he didn't want to bring me there because he lived in an all-colored neighborhood and I could get in trouble on his block?

And it works out. You know, in the lunchroom with all of those Spanish kids in one section, maybe sometimes a couple of colored boys we know are with us, or some of our Spanish boys might go over to their section. There are no racial riots between the Puerto Ricans and the Negroes there anytime I have been in the school. The only time there was any trouble was when a white person bothered a colored or Puerto Rican.

I guess it looks kind of funny there in the lunchroom. This section, Puerto Rican. Up here, Negroes. And in the middle, whites. Negroes might come down here. Puerto Ricans might go up there. But the white stay by themselves and they do it different.

An example: they bring their own lunch. They never eat the food from the school cafeteria and we always eat from the school cafeteria, or if we can, sometimes we sneak out for lunch. My mother made my lunch a couple of times. I liked it all right, but I couldn't trust myself to take it all the way to school. I don't know why the others bring their own stuff. I guess it's cheaper, but a couple of lunches were stolen once or twice and I decided that it would be better to buy it there.

Another boy used to play it real smart about that. He wanted to catch the crook that was stealing his food? So he put rat poison in it. He caught the guy all right. The guy was real sick. Had to go to the doctor. Oh, he got even, I mean.

You know, I like to get even just like everybody else. To get even. They stole my sneakers from out of my locker once and I went out and I stole five pair of sneakers. Five sneakers came out.

I don't know who took mine or whose I took. Look, they didn't even fit. But what I know is, I broke five lockers and stole five sneakers and I'm even. It didn't matter any more.

Another play like that worked good once. I had this crummy pair of coveralls. So I played a sob story with the teacher. You know, he said, when the laundry came back, he couldn't find my coveralls anywhere; couldn't understand it. Ha! So I told him that was the only pair I had and I couldn't afford any more money because . . .

And he says, "All right. We'll look for a pair for you." And then he gave me a brand-new pair of one of the teachers. And I was the only boy in that class with a teacher's uniform. I still have it.

The worst thing a teacher can do is to make a boy feel like he is losing his pride, something like that. They've done that to me lots of time. And there is nothing like it. I tell you, if I didn't have more self-control, I would probably beat up the teacher or knife him.

They can kill your pride. They make you feel like dirt and it's nothing nice to feel like. O.K., so you don't know something, you don't know it. But if you *do* know something, they give me an argument so good on it that they make you feel wrong even about what you *know*.

Let's take an example. Let's say, here I am talking about a car, about something wrong with the engine. And I know what's wrong with the engine because I have taken it apart and put it right, right in front of you. I tell you, "This is what is wrong with it. You can fix this part and the car will run." And he'll answer that the car will run without this part, or with it. If I tell him then that he's crazy, then it comes: "Don't tell me I'm crazy. I know what's going to happen. You're just a student, I'm a teacher, I'm better than you are."

The teachers can really hurt you if they want to. Like we had a teacher who would write up on the board before we even came in. All the boards would be filled with writing. And he wouldn't explain a thing to us. Every day the same thing—writing but no explanation for the things he wrote. And when the tests came, everybody failed.

And then he would criticize us, give us zeros, demerits and all these kinds of crazy things, and there was no way of getting to him. So we all got in a little group and went down to the principal's office. He didn't believe us. So what we did is, we stopped work. We never worked in that class and the teacher called the principal. We told him, "We won't work because he won't explain the things he writes up on the board and we can't learn unless he explains."

Finally they threw out that teacher and they brought in another one. That new one, all he ever did was explain. He never wrote anything on the board.

I mean, you get aggravated. All of these teachers are just too much for the boys. So there was only one way out. You play hooky, you cut out of that class, you sleep, you get even on him, you hate it. You live through it to get out of school.

Then you'd think a Negro teacher would be better, but one Negro teacher I had, she despised the Negroes and the Puerto Ricans more than anybody else. I guess some don't though. I had another Negro who liked us and was very kind and nice. Maybe it was just their own personalities.

My best teachers were mostly for English. They seemed to really want you to learn, they really strive for you to learn. Whereas most of the other teachers just don't care. They'll pass you either with a 65 or fail you with a 55. Good teachers are the ones that want you to get a high mark, and to join an honor class, like I was in. They really stress it; they really want you to go to it.

And with the kids, it's this way. Half of them want to learn and half of them don't. Half want to play around, whereas the other half, although maybe they do the same things, they *know* it's important. And on the sneak, away from the other boys, they study.

They don't want to let them know that they are *smart*. Well, you want to be somebody odd? I mean, everybody else is dumb. You have to be with the group.

Then there's another trouble. It's not really the language—most people know English. But you see, like even I do, it's the slang. You know, like instead of saying "officer," I say "cop." It's sort of something that gets into your head.

Like, if you are used to saying, "I ain't gonna do that," you know, and you go out into the street and that's all you hear from the people, "I ain't gonna do that, I ain't gonna sit over there."

Well, you go to school and the teacher says you aren't supposed to do that and the boys think she is crazy. I'm not going to go out in the street and talk like that. They won't believe me.

You know, in school you learn words and you read Shakespeare and you can't talk like that. There's some kid, he might know all of Shakespeare by heart, but when he gets out into the street, he can't talk to his friends like that; he can't talk to *anybody*. You have to use words that other people understand. Well, take a boy that can recite all of Shakespeare and all his plays—that kind of boy, one that can understand words that he hears in political speeches. He knows the words, the langauge, inside out. He'll soon get tired of the neighborhood where they only talk in slang or they only talk bad language. He won't have anyone to talk to. He will have to go and look for another kind of job, and he'll try to live in another kind of neighborhood where everybody talks in the fashion that he can understand; where, for once, he can just show what his real feelings are.

It's rough. How's a boy going to ever find out anything he has to know? The teacher says, "Does anybody not understand?" Well, he doesn't want to raise his hand and feel like an idiot, so he keeps his hand down and forty boys out of that class keep their hands down and forty boys at the end of the year won't graduate, or if they do, they won't know anything anyhow.

Like a new boy that was in our class. He, sort of like, he

showed that he was afraid at first, that he was little, that he had money. I remember the first day he came in here, they stole his watch. They stole his shoes and he walked around barefooted then. And me, I didn't feel sorry for him at all.

You know, with these kids, you learn how to handle them. You know what to do. If a boy comes in from a rich neighborhood, and he doesn't know how to handle himself, instead of asking for help, he goes right in there and really messes up the works. So he's bound to get beat up. He should stay to himself. If he stays to himself, he makes friends with one of the boys that he knows is good, he has it all right. But if he walks in there and he starts—you know—pulling out his money like this boy did, showing off his watch and answering—you know—answering all the questions in the class, oh, he was *dead*. I could tell, I didn't feel sorry for him at all because he was stupid.

The questions he would answer! It's not so wrong to answer some of them, but we would never answer *all*, tell *all* the answers because we wanted to leave something for the next day. If you answer all of them, the teacher would give you homework, you know. This boy was killing us, and he was so proud of it.

You know how it works. The teacher says to himself, "Well, you know this, I might as well give you some more." And we would never want more homework. So even if we know, we don't say, so as to have something else for the next day. Something a little left over. If you answer all of them, you're cooked. You get new work the next day and you might not know it and then you are really stuck. Stuck for the weekend.

Like that kid, he proved he had brains for the answers, but he didn't even make friends with anybody first. He was bothering everyone. All he had to do was make one snotty remark to anybody. Man!

He got beat up outside the school; practically every day for months it happened. As far as that goes, he didn't really have to do anything. Just go along minding his own business. Otherwise he'll have a lot of trouble.

And nobody helps. That's one good thing about our school. If they're all fighting one guy, unless you know the person that is getting it, you won't go into the fight. No matter how old, or how many, you let them.

And you know why I let them? Because it's happened to me so many times and if it hadn't happened to me, I would finally have been like maybe the boys in those other houses near me, in my neighborhood, afraid to fight, afraid of being hit, afraid of walking down the street alone at night. Afraid of coming out of their high-class hole in the ground.

Now, today, when I'm almost out of the whole mess, I know I'd rather have been in an academic course. To be able to go to college. Ah—a college degree is much better because I'd have more opportunities open to me. But if I want to go to college now, so late in school, there are bad things that I have to say.

What happened is, when I was in the ninth grade, my guidance counselor told me to be a vocational student. She said that I had the aptitude to be an auto mechanic. I think what must have happened is that some business guy must have called up that day to say that there was getting to be a shortage of garage mechanics—and to train a few jerks so he wouldn't have to pay too high salaries.

Anyhow I got here to a vocational high school, and when my marks were so good they put me in academic classes. You see in a vocational school, when a kid does good, an academic class is like an honor class. Now I'm taking a trade, auto mechanics, so that makes me a vocational student. Then, I'm taking honor classes. So I'm not getting the right training for my vocational course and I'm not getting enough training for my academic course. I'm sort of like in between. So if I want to go to college, I'm going to have to take extra courses at night school. Probably after I'm out of school and working I'd have to take night classes for years before I could even apply to college.

Even if I wanted to become a garage mechanic, I'm going to be in the same spot. I'll have to see if I can gain experience by watching after I'm working and just hoping that I'll learn. I've only had half a course of that, too. I'm just going to have to make my own way.

My mother, she wants me to go to college. She says the only good jobs are for college students and she tells me she doesn't want me to be a laborer. But she couldn't dish out money for my books, my expenses. She doesn't have to go through what I would. You know how hard it is to stay in college. If I have to be studying during the day time and in the late hours of the night, I can't see working. I'll be killing myself if I started working like something in the middle of the night.

Then, when I figure it all out, I see how much trouble I am going to have. You see, in college you would need a lot of math and I haven't had math since the ninth grade. I can't take it because at night you are only allowed to take one subject if you are still going to day school and I've been taking advanced English there in the night school. So, when I get to college, I guess math will be very hard for me. I was thinking about this last year one time and once, when I delivered some groceries down the street to a woman who lived there, we got to talking and I told her this trouble. So she began teaching me algebra, but it just got to a point where I couldn't take algebra any more.

It wasn't the algebra I guess, it was her house and her. Her house was too beautiful for me. I felt like a creep coming from my house to her house.

You know how those houses are? The patios and everything like that? And everything is carpets on the floor. Those people can afford everything. Whereas in my house it is a little more roomy now than we used to have it, but it's still not the same way as over there. So when I walk over to her house, I say to myself, "Why can't I have it like this? Why do I have to live over there?"

So then I say to her, "Well, I'll see you," but I know I'm not going back, that's all.

That woman, if I asked her to lend me a book she would tell me, "Well, it costs me thirty-five dollars. You have to come over here and read it and be sure not to damage the pages."

By that time I was ready to break the damn book over her head. You know, I would say she was helping me because she wanted to show her power. She was a good teacher, and maybe she wanted to pass it on, but I couldn't stand that thing about her money. The way she said it, like she was daring me to take her money, you know? More than anything else she talked about that. I'd get mad and kind of disgusted.

I'd say to myself, "Why couldn't my parents have afforded this? Why do I have to work and sweat? For what? For what *they* have."

Maybe, maybe if I work like a dog in school and later, my children will have it good. But I could have had it good if my parents would have done it first.

And then sometimes I envy them because they get to go all over. You know, they get to do everything and I can't, I'm only limited. Oh, in true form I don't show all this, I don't let it out. I hold it in, just like all the other people in Harlem hold it in, until it's too late and before anything happens, I leave.

Oh, not all teachers are like her. I had one very good teacher, in school. He was smart, too. He's young though and maybe he doesn't know as much as the old teachers who have been around for a long time and it shows in one way. He can get very hot-tempered, you know? And when he gets hot-tempered he really wants to smash somebody, though he doesn't do anything.

I guess he gets mad that he has been studying all this time to be a teacher and there are kids there, a whole class full, that don't want to learn, and I guess everybody would get mad at that. Like if you study to be a mechanic and nobody wants to bring their car to you, then what's the use? You know?

Like sometimes, him and me, right there in the class we start discussing something back and forth about history or like that. All right, it's good; we're both swinging. But those other kids, back there, in the back of the class? They are playing around. They're throwing papers at each other, or they're cursing, or they are talking about something else, or they're sleeping.

Like in hygiene, half of the kids are asleep. Or maybe even some of them drunk even before they came to school. A kid might sit there in the back of the class and he's a little bit up, you know. He thinks he's well off, but he's not. And he comes to school on a little tightrope. And before he gets to his third class, he's *out*.

All right, so that kid gets transferred, and another kid flunks out, and another kid drops out. A few of us stay and maybe

77

we get to graduate, but it doesn't do much good. Nobody has the right training; most of them, even when they graduate, can't read or write too good. They can't go to college; they haven't got the right training for a trade. Sometimes I think of going into the Navy because there, I'd get more training. I could go into the motor service and maybe learn to be a better mechanic. Anyway, I can study there. I mean, if I can't leave the post, go play pool or go with girls, there is only one thing I can do, I can study. Maybe in the Navy I'll have a chance.

Even if I could, by taking courses at night and get some money help, I think I'd have a big problem with college. I don't know how I would respond to it. College is a whole new thing. Maybe I wouldn't do so good. Suppose I would flunk out after all this time of struggling and working and wishing. I think maybe I better cool down a bit before I go.

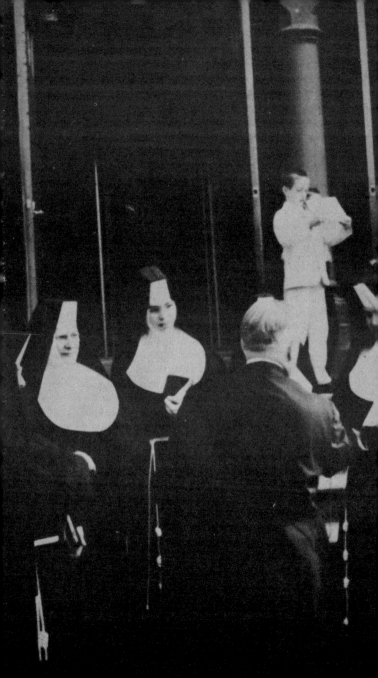

For elementary school I went to Holy Family, which is connected with our church. I knew all the kids in my school because I'd grown up with them. From the sandbox to the school together you could say, and, of course, a lot of them are still my closest friends, even though we don't all go to the same high schools now. Some of them go to private day schools, a few to other Catholic high schools, one or two to public schools and, one or two are away at prep school.

But generally, we're really the same happy family we were at elementary school. I still see the younger priests from the school at club meetings and around the church, and all of us who went to school together still sit around and talk about our school work now and the problems that we've got. One young priest whom I'm still very close to has really helped me with my Latin, even though I go to a different school now.

The year I graduated, I was a little worried about leaving Holy Family because it was so familiar and comfortable to me. But after I got to St. Brendhan's I found that it was easy to make friends. It seems that everybody was afraid in the freshman year. You were eager to make friends and get some self-confidence, and you found that it was easier to face school in freshman years with friends to talk over your problems with. Since everybody was in the same boat, it worked out very well without any troubles. Parents gave parties, we studied together, ate lunch in groups, and got over the strangeness.

Another reason I was so afraid before I got to the school was because of what my brother had told me about it. He went to the school and he warned me that it is very tough, and that you really have to work hard. I was afraid I wasn't going to work hard enough and that the teachers would be too strict. But now I see what a very good school it is. I was only thirteen when I came, though I have to admit that even now I'm a little scared the night before school begins each year. But that's natural; everybody dreads it at the beginning of the year.

Then the school really is very hard. It's all college preparatory and academically it's very tough. *Tons* of boys flunk out every year. For example, in this year's senior class there are 95 boys, but when they were in freshman year, there were 206. They just cut it in half, keep chopping it up. The kids who flunk out have to go to public high schools because it's very hard, once you flunk out of a Catholic high school, to get into another. One or two private schools might take you, but it would be much more expensive.

The system works like this: if you fail three or four subjects at midterm, you usually are forced to withdraw. If you fail two subjects at the end of the year, you have to withdraw or else repeat those subjects in summer school. That's your last chance, though. If you fail both of those in summer school, out you go.

I get pretty good scores in all my classes, but the thing I do worst in is World History. It isn't that it's so hard as that it's so dull. I suppose part of the problem is that both of my teachers in world history I hated with a real passion. I couldn't stand them. I didn't like their voices, I didn't like the way they spoke, they bored me completely. And both of them had their own little movements, or idiosyncrasies. One day, when last year's teacher was at his worst, I counted how many times he put his finger into his collar to pull it out—67 times!

He's a lay teacher, though that isn't to say that the lay teachers in my school are all worse than the Brothers. But all the Brothers are at least good workers. They're dedicated. This history teacher was—and I have to say it—just a lazy slob. He'd come into the room and sit down very sarcastically, putting his books on the table. It's possible to sit down sarcastically, if you try. You know, he'd look at you as if to say, "Isn't it too bad that *I* have to do all this for you?" A good example of how he taught is the section we had on the French Revolution. You'd think that it would take at least two weeks to cover the French Revolution, if you really want to do it. He covered it in one day, and he said that we really didn't have to know the rest. Well, in a way he was right because we took the Regents and we all passed, but we wanted to know more about it than just enough to get by. That wasn't the right attitude.

My Latin teacher is completely different and he is quite

good. He could get across what he wanted to, and if you followed him, you could pick up very easily what he meant to be saying, because he made it so simple. Of course, he had a short temper and if a kid was caught talking more than once during his class, he'd take him outside and bop him once or twice. I know that Latin will help me in later life to coordinate different things. For instance, you have five declensions, four conjugations. I've learned about eight thousand words in these two years so far, and every word you look at has got to be broken down into a declension, fitted into a verb, and all the rest. It shows you how to organize and how to collate one thing into another, to have it adjust.

I don't know my Latin well enough yet to enjoy the stories because by the time I translate them into English, Jason and the Argonauts and stuff like that don't sound too well. Then Caesar really stabs me! *"Caesar, himself,* with his troops on his left wing—*Caesar, himself,* walking down the road." What a bore, what a character!

By the time we graduate we have to know Latin, two modern languages, mathematics, science, history, economics and religion. It's a very full program.

So far I'm keeping up and getting pretty good scores, but I have to work very hard at it because to get into college, into Notre Dame, now is even harder than when my father and brother went. My brother wrote to them for me and they told him that I have to have at least an 85 average. Now that might be easy in some public school, but not at St. Brendhan's.

The one subject that really comes easy to me is English. Not the grammar, but the literature. Now we're reading Steinbeck and Hemingway and I liked Steinbeck the best of anyone I've ever read. He's really great. You really see life with him and the stories are fun to read.

For English this year, our teacher is a very smart man. I guess he must be about forty or forty-five, but he seems very young. He's really well qualified with a Ph.D. from a good university, and I look forward to listening to him, just like going to the theater or something. His background really shows.

Of course, everything depends upon the teacher—the amount of homework, what you learn, the discipline. And it's a funny thing about the teachers. For example, the Brothers at the school are very different from the priests at church. They're more like us, less pious you might say. They're almost always very sport-loving and they like to shoot the breeze and stay around and talk to us. Then, when you get into the classroom, most of them have completely different personalities. In the classroom almost every teacher I have is very strict and pays attention to his duties as a teacher.

Of course, like everybody else, teachers have their good days and bad. For example, I have one teacher for religion and geography, one class in the morning, the other late in the afternoon. Well, if he's had a bad day, by the time our afternoon class rolls around, we'll have a terrible period.

One day not too long ago was one of those bad days and it also happened to be the day that I didn't bring a test paper into class which I was supposed to have my father sign. I really was afraid to show it to my father because of the low mark, so I just put it away in my drawer and didn't take it home. Well, Mr. McCloskey said to me, "Mr. Quinn, do you have your test paper?"

I said, "No, Sir." And he told me to get outside. Well, when we got out there in the hall he asked, "What's your excuse, Mr. Quinn?"

I answered, "No excuse, Sir."

"All right, son. Take it like a man, Mr. Quinn, don't cry. Here's the strap."

Well, I got hit five times and it really hurt. Most of the time the teachers use the strap or a "magic baton." It's rubber or leather or something like that and every experience I've had with it—well, it's the worst pain I've ever experienced.

But I think it is a very good method, even though it's painful at the time. Because my Latin teacher last year, Mr. Raymond, told us about a man who is in an institution now, because he was driven literally crazy by some of the kids in his class. I think that this way, we really learn right from wrong and don't waste too much of our school time fooling around.

Of course, if a teacher is shouting at you or hitting you when you haven't done anything, and everybody else knows that you haven't, a boy will answer and try to prove his point in a polite way. But I've noticed that if a kid has really done what the teacher says he has, he will never talk back because then if he's found out, the teacher would kill him.

The system is really very fair, and everybody just accepts it. There was only one time when I saw the whole thing backfire, and it's the only time I ever saw a kid talk freshly or get out of hand with one of the teachers. We had one teacher last year who was really giving the kids a tough time. There was a boy in our class who was colored and—I don't know—I think that that teacher has a little bit of prejudice in him. So, when the boy was talking in the back of the class, Mr. Phalen told him to shut up. Well, the boy didn't like being spoken to like that and he just kept on talking. Mr. Phalen blew up. He walked down the aisle and picked the boy up by the collar and by the tie and gave him the back of his hand across the face. The boy dropped over the desk. Then, he got up very fast, closed his fist, and hit Mr. Phalen right in the chin.

Everyone was shocked, even the teacher for a moment. The boy, I think, just didn't know what he was doing and hit back without thinking, but he was expelled because this had never happened in our school before and they wanted to make sure that it never did again.

Generally, everybody gets along all right together in my school. Of course, it's all Catholic, mostly Irish and Italian. When my brother went to the school, I guess it was almost all Irish but that has changed a little. There are one or two Puerto Rican kids in the school and one or two Negroes, but that is not because there is any prejudice. The tuition is very high, considerably higher than other high schools. And, of course, it's very hard to keep up academically.

I've noticed about the two colored boys in the school that nobody troubles them and they don't trouble anybody. We all get along. They stick to themselves, but we all talk together once in a while. For example, when we have intramural sports, one of the boys is on the basketball team and on the tennis team. As a matter of fact I taught him how to play tennis in the first place. Both boys are very good, very nice. I see them to talk to walking from school to the subway station, but that's about all. Generally they stick to themselves.

When I graduated from Holy Family, there were two Negro boys in my class and more in the other classes. And there were about four Puerto Ricans in the same year. Now, of course, you see more colored and more Puerto Rican there. They come mainly from the projects because if a child is a Catholic and if his parents register him, he can go to the school. There's only a small book fee, and a very small fee for the year, so that anybody can afford it. When I was at Holy Family, though, color didn't matter very much. How can I put it? There didn't seem to be any racial problems or anything then, like I hear there are now. The kids just got along nicely. But they were comparatively good kids, most of those who went to our school. They didn't have any of these aggressions or anything like that. We just figured a guy, whether he was good or bad, not by color or anything like that.

The only time there was ever any trouble was when exams were coming along near the end of school and everybody was terrified. We were all so scared that we'd take it out on each other once in a while. But it wasn't that one group would gang up against another. No one ever used knives or anything like that when I went there.

Now, at St. Brendhan's, we just don't have the problem, although the school is open to any boy who can make it. I don't know, I may be wrong about how many colored and Puerto Rican boys there are. Maybe there are one or two more that I don't know, or that I never get a chance to speak to.

Another reason we all get along so well at school is that everybody has the same ideas about the future. About 99 per cent of the boys in my school are planning to go to college. Of course, they have different colleges in mind; some want to go to Georgetown; some who don't have too much money might go to Iona; others go to almost any school in the United States. I feel like there is only one school for me and that is Notre Dame. My uncles all went there, my father, brother, three or four of my cousins. It's the thing that worries me most about my grades—whether they are high enough to get into

Notre Dame, and whether I'll do well enough on the College Boards to get into Notre Dame.

In a way, I wish it was all behind me and that I was settled down. I used to think that I would like to be an engineer, but I find that I'm having some trouble with math and I have to get that straightened out before I make a real decision. I got the idea of engineering because I enjoyed geometry so, but now I see that that was just a special case.

When I look at my father and my brother I realize that they have a career that is very challenging. What I want is a job that would not be just the same drab routine, nine to five every day. I think the thing I would like would be a very good sales job for a large corporation, where you're not tied to an office. I hate being tied to a seat over a desk for a long time. I would go out of my mind if I had to do that all my life. Then, my father loves his profession. He enjoys talking about it and is always telling his friends and family about his job, about the products and how they're manufactured and the good orders that he's gotten. My father has risen to be vice president of a big company and we are very proud of him, but the best part about it is that he likes it so much. He finds his work very interesting and he seems to have such joy in making friends in the business and telling us about it.

The kind of sales job I would like would need a good college degree the way my brother and my father have. My brother told me an experience of his, when he got his job. He went to a large company's personnel office and there was a line of men waiting to apply for a very good position. Well, the secretary came out of her office and asked if there were any college graduates. There were three men who put up their hands, plus my brother, and they were ushered in, given great treatment, and allowed to apply right there. My brother got a job from them without any trouble about a week later while all the other people sitting out in the waiting room never even got a chance to tell their qualifications.

College would give me a lot more, too. I think you are much more worldly minded and know more about people if you're a college graduate. Usually you take psychology and sociology and you know how to cope with people and with life much better.

I just hope that I get into Notre Dame. It *is* much harder now, but I guess the fact that all my family has gone there will help a little. And I know I couldn't get a better start than what I'm getting at St. Brendhan's.

# Politics

Many of these conversations took place
between the time President John Kennedy
was assassinated and the 1964 Presidential
race between President Lyndon Johnson and
Senator Barry Goldwater. Juan is always
very aware of the political scene. He spends
a lot of time talking about politics and
trying to work out for himself a political
philosophy appropriate to his own situation.
He listens to speeches, is always "looking for
a fight" about the latest political development,
and frequently asks for information about
political figures with whom he is unfamiliar.

Peter is not interested in politics or in
government in any theoretical sense. He has
participated in some of his family's political
activities on the local district level and he is
interested in politicians or officials with whom
he can personally identify. He was extremely
disturbed by President Kennedy's assassination
and he is still very moved when he refers to it.

# Juan Gonzales

Whenever I hear a political speech or something like the Governor is not quitting, he's going to go on running, or things like that, I don't understand what it is all about. But pretty soon I start thinking.

You know I felt bad when Kennedy was assassinated because that's wrong, to kill anybody. But I figured out that all the people that have a lot of money are the ones that are in politics. You see in the news all the time that another Rockefeller goes into politics or a Kennedy. Those are the only people that can get anywhere and I can't see it. It's supposed to be that the people, they govern themselves. But it seems as if the rich guy controls all the others. They move and we follow. We pay taxes and they get rich and that is all wrong.

Abraham Lincoln's supposed to be very poor, and poverty-stricken, and finally he worked himself up to be the President of the United States. Anybody that's poor *now* couldn't get in. Like, they showed a picture of Johnson on his ranch or someplace. He didn't go there by car. He didn't go there by bus. He didn't go there by train. He went there by helicopter. Now how many people do you think can afford a helicopter? Who could afford a limousine? That just tells me that the rich man is running the government.

And even the Puerto Ricans who managed to get elected to something, they never can get to the point where they can say to anybody, "Do this, do that." They can only get to the point where their own ignorant people, the Negroes and the Puerto Ricans, can say, "Well, we have somebody up there now. We can really tell the big shots what we want." But they are really like nowhere. It is just the same as if they were still out on the street saying, "I want my rights."

Now I don't believe in the Nazi Government or anything like that, but I believe that once the poorer people get to a stage where they can just *take* their rights, *that's* when the people will run their government.

Like that class stuff? It's really color that's class now. If the

Negroes weren't Negroes, if they were all white, if there were all whites in the world, the upper class couldn't have any way to keep so much power.

Now, we have people going around saying, "Oh, look at that colored guy. I don't want to see him with a white woman." Things like that. This is where you get your problems, your riots.

And nothing helps so far. Even Malcolm X, he starts a campaign, but then he doesn't go all the way through. He leaves the Negroes hanging on a string, just dangling. He says he's going to do something, but all of a sudden he changes his mind and goes to something else.

But anyway, Malcolm has a problem. He organized the Negroes, but then they wouldn't go behind him. They wouldn't help him, so Malcolm himself was left there hanging. He thought he was leading a group and all of a sudden he found there was nobody there. Everybody was home, criticizing, or getting criticized.

Like when you have those sit-down strikes. All right, so you get a little, maybe even a lot, of newspaper stories out on it. But what is it doing for them? Nothing. They are only being arrested and they are being put in jail and their money's being taken away from them. They are being *destroyed*. What chance can a Negro or a Puerto Rican have if he goes to school? He can't get where the power really is. Like he can't go into the Treasury Department or into the Defense Department or be a general. He can't go like to be working as a Secretary of State.

Well, I figured out that the Negroes, since they *are* segregated, if they would form a group all by themselves, but with the Puerto Ricans, then they could try to get money, power. They could form into a great empire. You see, then no one could tell them, "Do this, do that." They'd be on their own.

The way it is now, what's the use of having a Negro who's a genius? They won't give him a chance to work. What's the use of having guys, Negro guys, that can solve diseases? If he does solve them, then someone else takes the credit. It's no use for the Negro unless he gets organized. I'm not saying that they'd be better off living someplace off by themselves. I'm saying that they should stand up for their rights, get something done for themselves. Live in *this* society, but, I mean, why plead to the whites when the whites close their ears to them? Why don't they plead with the others who are down? Why doesn't the Negro say to the Puerto Ricans, "Why don't you help us? Why don't you join us and get something done about the things that we both want? Why don't you help us get more money? Why don't you help us get more power? Why don't you help us get credits and distinctions so you know who's who?"

But, you know, that's tough. Like, I've never met any Puerto Rican kid who thinks on his own the way I do. Like I'm alone.

That's because the Puerto Ricans and the Negroes hold everything back. Because they fear if they say something it's just that they'll be hurt and be hurt bad. They're afraid. They know what's what. No one wants to listen.

O.K., say a lot of people start to say, "Well, here are these boys, fifteen- sixteen-year-old boys, if they can go on strike for their rights, why shouldn't we help them?"

Well, maybe some people do say that, but most of them are not going to listen, they're just going to lay back and die. These strikes or these boycotts don't have any effect. The people with power, they hear, and maybe some of them are losing money, but they are not really getting hurt that bad. If a Puerto Rican who has a job went on strike, didn't make money, he'd die. He couldn't support himself or his family and sooner or later he'd just perish. They'd be nothing left for him. A person of the upper brackets, he can go on a one-man strike. Just do what he wants. He would lose out in the little business profit, or maybe close down one business, but he'd still have another chain there.

Then, another thing, people with a lot of money have everything they want. They've got money, power, but that's not enough for them. They want to be able to know that their grandchildren will see their name written down in a book someplace, as Governor, as President. They want something to be remembered by, but that doesn't mean that they are qualified to be a leader. You can have a Puerto Rican over here and really he's not making over $2,000 a year, but he can have the experience enough to go over there and run the government.

But what happens now? A guy who's got the money starts campaigning and gets a big job. He doesn't have to know a thing about it. Then, on the other side, you have someone like me. I can know everything about politics, but I can't go and start a campaign. I don't have the power. I could say some thing to my people, to Negroes, but until I get some power I just have to keep my mouth shut.

You know, I never had a lot of money, I don't know how I would react with power. But I don't think I would look down on my own. Let's put it this way: if I am a middle-class person who has enough power to make me want to go mad, I think I would do right and bring in more Puerto Ricans here and try to get them higher. I wouldn't leave the Puerto Ricans flat. I would try to bring them up. But people don't do that.

Puerto Rican politicians are more crooked than even the cops because you see they are up there, maybe one Negro, one Puerto Rican, among all those whites. They don't know what's going on, they feel dumb. They feel dumb and they are treated dumb even though they are all politicians together. The whites, they give that one poor slob all the lousy things to do. He takes orders and he obeys them. Whatever the white politicians want, the Negro or the Puerto Rican goes through with it. I don't think until another generation will you find a Puerto Rican politician that can think on his own, to go out there and do his job, as if for his own people. Now he'll do what the others want him to.

The only one who's got power is Adam.* You can see that they listen to Adam Clayton. He came to our school once and he gave a long speech and every kid there applauded. We believe in what he says because he has power, maybe not as much as the other people up in Congress, but enough to try to help.

Not like Malcolm X.** He has no power. He can't even get

*Adam Clayton Powell, Congressman from New York. Mr. Powell is a Negro.
** Malcolm X, Negro nationalist leader, was assassinated in February, 1965, several months after this conversation.

the people behind him. And instead of trying to think his way out of a problem, he uses the gun, and the fists, and riots. That's how all of this riot problem came up. There is nothing in Harlem now. All the wars, breaking up the stores. Now that's stupid. I mean, what do they get out of it? Usually the people that have the stores are the whites. I guess they figure that they will hurt the whites by breaking up their little companies, but it just gets the Negroes into trouble.

You know, kids are more restless than old people. The old people can afford to wait, they are used to it. But the younger group, they say, "Well, we've got to do it now, because when I grow up I want to be able to walk down the street free. I don't want to walk, like down the street, a slave."

And the shooting of that kid before the riots got them mad. First of all, a policeman is supposed to give a person a warning shot. If he is going to shoot, he shoots at the legs and he won't kill the person. Now I know it didn't happen like the cops say. I can't see a little boy, fifteen years old, grab a knife and try to attack an officer. Now that's not easy to believe. I'd be scared to attack an officer with a knife, when I know the cop had a gun. I don't believe that cop was telling the truth.

But, really, that shooting didn't have anything to do with the riots. It just set off the fuse. Harlem was tensed up because they got their civil rights bill, but they were still going backwards. They were still being treated like privileged savages and so they finally said, "Well, let's be savages. I mean, they treat us like savages, we might as well become savages."

And where does it get them? Have you heard from Adam Clayton lately? Nothing. How can he help when they are in these riots. Can he say that his people are nervous? He can't say nothing. He can't help them just because they are rioting. If they keep it up, they are just going to get themselves in a lot of trouble. You notice you didn't see many Puerto Ricans out that night because the Negroes can't sometimes tell a Puerto Rican from a regular white person in the middle of the night, when it's dark, unless the Puerto Rican talks up. But the Puerto Rican can get out of hand just as well as the Negroes. Now, the Negroes are just out, and the whites are stopping them, but suppose, all of a sudden, suppose the Puerto

Ricans went out of hand, too. They would be too much to handle and if the Puerto Ricans and the Negroes ever join up, they'll be like a revolution.

The trouble is that nobody is looking ahead, everybody's looking out for now. And I just watch, and I just see how everything's going and I am making plans to move out of this little city, because I know there's going to be a lot of more trouble. There's just the beginning now. Everybody thinks the worst has ended, but the worst hasn't even shown up yet.

I have never enjoyed politics much. I've watched the news almost every night for years and I've listened to the commentators asking politicians questions about current events. I have never yet experienced a straight answer from any of them, and I just don't like that.

The only time I ever had much to do with the whole subject was when my uncle ran for district leader. That was fun. I got my friends and my cousins and we put up signs and stuff like that. I didn't pay too much attention to the political part of it and though I was disappointed that he didn't get in, I have to say that the part I liked best about the campaign was climbing lampposts to get the signs up.

The only election I ever paid much attention to was when Kennedy was running, but I don't consider that politics. I said to myself then, "If Kennedy isn't going to be elected, I want to die." I really went for him because he was Irish, because he was Catholic, because he was so very good in politics, I thought. Everybody I knew or spoke to liked him and didn't like Nixon. Then, when he got in, I was very proud to see him there, and he was doing a great job. He put a lot of new things in and tried for many things that Eisenhower would never even think of. My father took me to see him once when he was coming into New York and that was the greatest thrill of my life.

Then—well—I guess I'll never forget the day he died. It was the last period in school and we were doing our geometry homework and then Brother Joseph, the principal of the school came over the P.A. System and said, "Attention, stop everything and listen. Very important." And then a radio came on and through the microphone a voice said, "We have confirmed that the President died." He was dead and everybody was stunned. I was terrified. I was really afraid. I said that the world was going to come to an end and I kept thinking about it and thinking about it and I was really more afraid than I have ever been in my life or than I ever will be.

The thing that got me was how he could be killed by such a small man. How such a small creature could really ruin us, could really shock the whole nation, how easily this could be done. I felt that way for a long time, but then when I saw what kind of person Johnson was I got over it.

That day everybody thought it was a joke, they were too shocked to believe it. The school was very quiet. Usually there's a lot of hustle and bustle after the day is over with everybody throwing books around and going crazy, but that day nobody said anything.

Then, when I watched the funeral, I was terribly depressed, and yet I was very proud of how all that honor was given to the President, to someone who came out of the same background as I did. Everybody really loved him. So many heads of state and leaders of other countries came, and it really struck me when the caisson came out of the White House through those gates and all the heads of state walked together in a crowd as if they were no one compared to Kennedy. Just for this man. Then they all attended Mass and it was really beautiful. I was proud of the Presidency and how it was and, then, remembering him, I felt terrible.

As a matter of fact the only time I ever paid any attention to political speeches was during that campaign. Now, I don't pay much attention because politicians always get around the questions and never really say much. But that Kennedy-Nixon debate, that was the greatest! Nixon was falling all over himself and I loved it.

In this last campaign that we had for President, I was for Johnson, but my family was not. We didn't talk much about it, but I was worried about some of the things that Goldwater said he would do. They were really wild. I never discuss it much with my brother because he generally approves of Goldwater and I know that if I got into a big discussion with him I don't know enough. If I had a fight with him, a mental fight, I would be only half armed.

I don't think much of Johnson either, but about war he seems to be more sensible. He's more or less following Kennedy's lead, though on a smaller scale. Kennedy showed, in the

Cuban blockade, that he wasn't taking any nonsense from anybody, though he wasn't recklessly dropping bombs.

Johnson is a hard man to like. I don't like his Southern way of speaking and that really bothers me. As for Humphrey, I can't stand him. He acts like a fool talking too much and not being dignified. He just doesn't seem to know how to behave.

The thing that really surprised me in the last election was that Robert Kennedy beat Senator Keating. I thought he was great and a very good politician, but that he wasn't going to win. I thought that Senator Keating had Senator Javits* on his side and the Jewish population would vote for Keating. I don't know why, but I expected all the Jews in New York to vote for him. Of course, all the Irish and all the Catholics always knew who they were going to vote for, not only because the Kennedys are Irish Catholics, but because they knew that Bobby was a very good organizer and someone who would carry on his brother's program.

I suppose it's only natural to be glad to see one of your own group in a high office. Not everybody has that chance. For example, I think there would be very small chance for a Puerto Rican person to reach a really important position in government. I suppose you can achieve something, if you're good enough, through contributions, but it takes an awful lot of money to go through politics and someone who just starts out with nothing would have to work awfully hard. Usually, politicians have some resources of their own. Just look at other politicians as an example. Goldwater is worth 2 million, Johnson is worth 17 million, and the Kennedy family is worth something like 300 million. To get where they are takes a lot more than any Puerto Rican or Negro has right now.

Although everybody in this country has a chance to run for office, probably a Negro or Puerto Rican now wouldn't be accepted. He has the right, but I don't think he can be elected. I suppose if the major party had very good faith in a Negro they might let him come in, but they'd have to have a very good idea that he'd win and that wouldn't happen very often. Another problem is it would be harder to find a Negro that

* Senators from New York, 1964. Jacob Javits is Jewish; Kenneth Keating, who was defeated by Robert Kennedy, is not.

was educated or qualified enough. I'm not saying that they are dumb people; they just haven't had the opportunities because we haven't given it to them. Maybe, sometime, there will be a time when they are ready. Fifty years from now.

But I don't spend too much time thinking or talking about politics. I guess there are some things that politicians could do, like cleaning up the slums and living conditions. Or something that bothers me personally, is that there ought to be more privileges for the teen-age boy in New York. For example, there are places to play now, but they're not nearly large enough, so that if a team wants to play hard ball without getting into some organized league, there are very few fields that are big enough. It would be nice if someone were to take care of that kind of thing, but I don't think that I've ever even talked about it to anybody.

I have one friend, though, who really can talk. We're always telling him that he is going to be a lawyer when he grows up. Once we got into a quarrel on the street with some man who just came up to us and began talking about Goldwater and saying that Goldwater would ruin the government. We were just sort of ignoring him, but when our talking friend came over he jumped right into that guy. He pointed a finger right in the guy's face and said, "You're a Commie." It seems that there was a picture of a man in the paper recently who was a Communist, and it looked just like this man. Maybe it even was. And my friend demolished that fellow and he went away without having much more to say. John's really a great talker, about any subject.

But it's not something we argue about or get all excited about. Even in my own family my father, brother, and sister are for Goldwater; my mother is for Johnson. Nobody ever quarrels about it, though, no worries.

# Goals and Ideals

In the course of his very spotty and sporadic after-school reading, Juan has come across such things as a biography of Adolph Hitler, some Marxist slogans, a book on teen-age gangs (which he considered foolish). One sees their influence on his ideas which change frequently as do Juan's goal and ideals.

Peter has well-defined educational plans, but his ideas about a career change from time to time. He talks very often about his anxiety about getting into the college his father and brother attended which, at the moment, is his chief goal.

Both boys frequently refer to the rioting which took place in New York City and elsewhere during the summer of 1964. They are both very conscious of racial tension in America and in New York in particular.

# Juan Gonzales

I think about what I should do when I get out of school, and I just don't know. The people in my neighborhood, in Harlem, or downtown, they're all doing it wrong. And if one tries to get out, the rest laughs. Like they say that they tried and couldn't do it, so you're not going to do it either. And this guy feels, "Well, maybe I can't do it," and he comes back into the slum. You figure, you know, they failed, man, I might as well give up.

I mean, even someone like Adam Clayton. O.K., maybe he studied as a child. I guess to be a Congressman, it doesn't matter how much money you got, you got to be doing your stuff. But maybe that money his father had, helped him, because maybe his father gave him special things. You know, private school, things like this. Or maybe he never once had even to *go* to a slum area.

And that's the thing that gives a feeling of inferior. It tells a person that no matter how hard they try, they can't get out. That's the whole thing right there. I mean a rich person wouldn't have to go around mugging people, or robbing them. The trouble really is down at Harlem, because Harlem is a place where you don't get anything of anything. That's where, like you used to live when you didn't have nothing. And until you get something, you'll never get out of that place.

If I could start fresh, do anything in the world, I would like to live in a place where it wouldn't be crowded, where it wouldn't have 20 million people walking up and down the street. I don't like living in the city, I want to live in the country. I think when people are further away from each other they can have more peace. When you're crowded in like this, you're worried. You're worried that your child's going out into the street and he's going to get killed.

Living in a project, we can't do anything; it's not ours. With all of this, if you have a house in the country, that's your own. You have it for yourself. You have enough to keep you happy. You have enough food there and enough good food to get by. You could be out there feeling free and gay.

I mean you would be free. You would know that you're not in any political strife, that you have no segregated problem. I am alone and I am enjoying it. Because you don't want to be bothered with these problems, you don't want to be bothered like crossing the street, or walking somebody else's turf. You don't want to be bothered by anything. You just want to be left alone. Maybe a couple of people you'd like around—out there by myself with a couple of friends, maybe a girl, you still have enough fun with each other. You get along.

But when you put all the people up together under one roof, they just don't get along. They dispute and argue. If you could move wherever you want, and if there was no money and nobody to bother you, I would build my house in a nice spot in the country in the shade of the trees. You know everybody thinks of a paradise for themselves and I think that's mine.

But I know I could never have it. First, it costs too much and I don't have any money; and two, I don't think there's a place in the world where you can go and be alone and you can get away from all the troubles in the world.

I like a couple of friends, for company, but there's really nobody, like, you could say I look up to, I admire, in this world. Only Napoleon, or Hitler. Not so much because of what they did, but I admire the way they came to power. I admire the way they got their power. Just think of Napoleon, this small guy you have there, everybody around is real tall, real important, and this guy says he's taking over. Think of it. He's just a corporal and he took over the government. That's what I admire. I admire a person who, when he wants something, he goes after it. Me, I don't do it. I don't do it.

Of course what Hitler did was wrong, killing everybody, destroying people. But you saw what he could do, how he constructed the army and things like that. If he could have done that, why didn't he use his power to create good things? He wouldn't have to go out and kill everybody else so that then they could be best, because his people were the only ones alive. He could have done something to keep his people best fit. Or he could have created a paradise out of Germany because of the way the people followed him. He took over so quickly, he so arranged it, that the people were willing to do anything for him and when you have people like this, you have to use them. You don't put them into weapons. You give some people weapons, they go out and kill every Jewish, or they go out and kill every Negro. I would try something else, to construct something, if I was in power, like Hitler.

But I really think he was right on one point; that you can't trust the people with power. Here in the United States you can't tell the people who are not educated to take over the government, because look what they'll do with it. They'll just make so much turbulence and destruction that you're going to find yourself without a government, without any kind of nation. Like even now, the people don't know which way they're going. The Puerto Ricans and coloreds don't know, the whites don't know. Say you see two boys fighting or yelling at a movie or something like that. People don't even have to turn around. They say, "Oh, well, that's the Puerto Ricans or the Negroes."

Well, if I'm sitting next to them, I kind of feel sad. I mean, how can you blame *them*? How can you blame *everything*? You can't blame everything on Puerto Ricans and Negroes. Well, the Puerto Rican or colored kid they blame it on wrong, they punish, they get even. He doesn't go out and beat up another kind of kid. He comes and he beats up a Puerto Rican or a colored kid just like himself. They don't have any reason. It's just because they're looking at themselves, sort of like a mirror of themselves. They want to take it out on themselves, being colored, so they go out and hurt somebody just like themselves.

I mean they can't help it. They're stuck. I'm not accusing the whole group of whites. But you take a couple of whites and anything that happens to them, their house can be robbed, or their daughters can be raped, or their sons can be beat up, and they won't ever bother to ask the police who did it. Right away, they say it was a Puerto Rican or Negro.

The trouble is a lot of times they're right. But what do they think? The Puerto Ricans and the Negroes have to get even for what this man does to them, they have to resort to violence. If the white man likes to see a picture in the movies, they start rioting in the movies. To get even. They want their rights, and if the white man is stopping them, they are going to make sure that white man moves aside, so they can get by. It doesn't have to be the same white person that did one thing; it just has to be the same kind of person—white—and they want to make him suffer.

Then, the other side, the white man, he's got to hold off these groups, and it's pretty hard for him. So, since he has the law on his side and everything else, he uses it against them. The thing begins again.

Like of all the Negroes and Puerto Ricans I know, none of them know any whites except social workers. And a real tough guy, he wouldn't go near the social worker. Because he'd feel that he is going to be changed, and he doesn't want to be changed. He wants to be able to be the same way he is, so he can tackle the world.

Then there's another kind of kid, like a boy in our building, about ten or eleven years old. He walks around with those boys from the other houses, kidding around in the park with them, and he *thinks* like them. But when he comes to our side, he thinks like us. His father and mother, they taught this boy everything. You know that he used to be able to read an *encyclopedia* at the age of nine? He could pick up an encyclopedia and read it through with no problem. But the trouble is, the parents don't want him to be around us, or with the rest of the people in our building. They want him to go over to the other side.

In a way they're doing right, and in a way they're doing wrong. When you think of it, why should he stay on our side when it's really better for him to stay on the other side? I mean, he's very intelligent. What can he do with our groups that don't even know how to spell all the words he pronounces?

And the other thing, there's a lot of boys in my building that are like animals. When they start playing around, they aim to hurt you. And that boy, he's not that strong or that big. He can get hurt very easily. He should stay on the other side where the boys play silly games. The little games that they play, we've grown them out. We never play them since we were very little. You know that they have those big parks near our house? Even so, you know where those boys play? They don't go near those big parks, they play out against the buildings. And why?

107

I would say they would play there like the little kids because they can't go across the street to our neighborhood. They think it's dangerous for them.

Ah—it is. They'd probably get beat up. Maybe if a boy is alone from across the street? They might stop him and ask him for a nickel or dime. And if they found he had it, they'd take the money from him and beat him up before they'd let him go, whether he had money or not.

I don't believe in that, to take money from a little boy. They used to do that to me a lot, you know. I was smaller at P.S. 305, the boys from 96 would come over and take all the money the little kids had, but I had a couple of fights and they started laying off. I never did it because I can't look into a little kid's eyes and ask for his money because I could feel him shivering and I don't like it.

But I don't know any boys from those big houses. As long as I'm living here, all the boys over there have been going to private schools and they're very snotty. They think they're way superior. They can't show it by a fight because they lose. They never fought, you know; they always had it easy. But if we went to the same school, they would show it. If I didn't have the answers to a question and I was wondering how to do a problem, Paddy boy wouldn't tell it. He would tell you, "Well, you're stupid. You don't know."

But we fix them up. We do the same thing they did to us. For once, we had something that they wanted and we wouldn't give it to them. Like questions, you know, girls' phone numbers, or to teach them how to fight, or how to make out. Things like that. They never had any girls. Those kids around there, they're locked up like in solitary. They don't even know what girls look like. Their mothers don't want them to get it because then, they will know. They want to get that little boy of theirs into a good family. They don't want to let him go around with the trash downstairs. I know that, but the boy, you know, he wants it. He still feels lonely, he wants to go around, wants to meet some of the girls.

And then you know something, the girls really go for him because he's different. At the same time some of them are disgusted with him, it depends. Like some girls that we introduced this one boy to, they generally went head over heels with him. But as soon as they heard him talk, they all walked away. Because he's snotty. He tries to make himself bigger than he really is. And it doesn't make sense. He's a nice-looking kid all right, but he should just keep it like that. As soon as he talks, he starts with the feeling, "I got more money than you have."

That's one good thing about it, I mean about the way things are with us. I get freedom, a lot more freedom than those other kids who live near us. If I want something, my parents will give it to me if they can. But if they can't give it to me, they know it's not going to kill me. Whereas with *those* boys, their parents would give him all kinds of different arguments on why they shouldn't have it.

Or another thing. I could go out any time of night, you know, if I felt up to it. I'm pretty sure that one of the boys in those houses couldn't go out as late as I could. Their parents think up excuses instead of just saying no. They want to tell the boy why he shouldn't go.

Let's say it's Friday night about nine o'clock, and I get all dressed up, and I say, "I'm going out to a dance," or to some-place like that.

*This* boy, if he was going, they would say, "Where are you going? How far is it away? How long are you going to stay away? Who are you going with? What are you going to do there? Are there gangs there? Bad girls?" And they might tell him when to come home, they might tell him not to drink. He wouldn't be able to do almost anything I would.

That boy, he doesn't go out much because they are not sure of him. They don't know what he is going to do outside. They are always walking with him. He has a lot of protection from his parents and then, when he is away from them, he doesn't know how to handle himself. I usually go all the time away from my parents and I do pretty well.

The way I see it, right now, I think I have it better than that other one. But when I was small, then he had it, and when I get *older*, he will have it still better. He will have a better education. He will have a better atmosphere.

Like I wouldn't be able to go to a rich night club, or hire a night-club singer, or have a good career. He might turn out to be a lawyer or a doctor or something, whereas I could only be maybe a mechanic or a machinist. I might make money, but I won't make the same kind of money he makes.

Even so, with the people that live in those houses, the parents tell their kids right from wrong, so the boy never knows right from wrong until he goes out into the world himself.

But with me, my mother always had affection, more affection than I think the women in that building. They just smother their kids. They make them like the Mama's boy. They say, "Well, don't go out too far. Be careful. Come back soon. Don't make me worry." So the boy might even be sixteen, seventeen, and he still is worrying about his mother. He still is hanging around her. Just taking all he can get. Not on his own, still living off his mother.

And about girls? With us, if a girl developed at twelve or thirteen years old, she was made. That's about the age. There were no girls belonging to the gang, but when a boy met a girl, she went around with other girls and the boys would know all of them. That's how we got around. We'd see each other like at private parties, something like that. Most of the time there were no adults around, and some of the boys would bring along something to get it going. Kids would be drinking and they'd go wild. At fifteen, I was something like what you would call one of those lovers. I was always walking around with the girls. That was the most exciting.

Sometimes I'd go to those Latin dances and sometimes I'd go to the dances at St. Mary's. I went there instead of Holy Family because I don't like that church or anything about it because of the priest there who did me. Even so, even at St. Mary's most every time there's troubles, fights. I mean, you know, you go over to dance with this girl you think is alone and the guy that brought her doesn't like it. Sometimes you push this one guy and you find out that he brought his whole gang with him. Your friends are not going to let you get beat up and disgrace the neighborhood. I mean, are you going to let this little gang beat you? Here you fought so many times?

Sometimes there are a couple of priests at a dance, but mostly there are men and women who are just watching out.

When a fight breaks out, they get out of the way. At first, they tried to stop it, but I mean how could you stop it? Everybody is in a gang. That's how come they usually went to these places. Some went to fight, some went to drink, some went to find sex, others just went to see what was going on. Mostly, what turned out were fights, sex, and drinking.

Some guys went in couples, but I could never see myself bringing a girl there because you'd probably lose her halfway through the dance, you know. You had to be watching this guy wasn't fooling around with your girl while he was dancing with her, things like that.

I don't think the priests know how much goes on, and if they do know, they keep it quiet. If it got out in the papers or somewhere, they'd put up such a fight. They'd say, "No, no, it never happened." Because nobody wants to discredit the Church.

Except me. I don't care any more. My mother was Catholic, but she got divorced and remarried, so they took her off the Catholic religion. She still cries about it sometimes, even though she goes to some other place now that has all religions in it. Whereas I won't go to any of them, I wouldn't go near a church.

My brother used to go, too, but now he's got the same ideas as I do. All of a sudden I thought it was so meaningless. You know? It was nothing there. My mother says that I should go, but I tell her I believe in myself and I believe that there's a Supreme Being and that if anything goes wrong it's because He wants it to go wrong. Nothing else.

I can't help what life is, I can only live it. Going to church is not going to do anything for me because there's thousands of people who go to church and they all come out cursing and believing in all kinds of sinful things. Some people, they could be in there praying for years and they come out of church and they get run over by a car.

Then, something happened that really made me see it. My house was robbed and the boys that were robbing, they were all caught. There was a lot of money stolen and everything, but the parents of these boys, they went to the church and they said, "Father, please help us out. Get our children out of jail."

So that priest went and he swore on the Holy Bible that these boys went to confession every week and they went to church every day, that they were holy and that anything that they were supposed to have done just wasn't true.

So, on the word of that priest, those guys were released. I went to see him. I went to confession and I went to see him, but you know, I didn't say anything. I just walked into the booth. I didn't even get down. I looked right at him and I asked him if he believed in God and he told me he did. Then he said, "Do you believe in God? That's the question."

I answered him. I told him, "I don't believe in God as long as you are a priest."

Then I went on and I told him everything, that he let some boys out of prison on false evidence and on false pretense. Those boys never went to church because I went to church and I never saw any of them. And because of him, who is never supposed to lie, they got away with it and they're probably going to hold up somebody else.

I said . . . right there in the confession booth I told him, "You lost yourself a customer. I'm never coming back here again. Because if *you* believe in God, *I* can't believe in God."

Oh, I used to believe in the Church. When I was a little boy I believed that when I did something wrong, the Church could cure anything. You know, by going to church and by praying to God, everything would be all right. It never turned out that way. It was always the same thing when I came out. Always lousy, always trouble.

Now I'm not going to bend to anybody's will. Now I see that when you pray, you're praying because you're scared, you're scared of what's going to happen, and you're scared of stopping from praying because you're afraid that the Lord might come down and strike you with a bolt of lightning or something. I feel really sorry for my mother in all this, her getting kicked out for remarrying, but I'm not going to go anyhow. I haven't gone at Easter and I guess that lets me out for them, too. My mother doesn't like it, but she doesn't like a lot of things.

Another thing that gives her worry with me is that she has a sort of pride about Puerto Ricans. When I first started talking English at home, my mother said, "You speak English outside, you talk Spanish in here!"

Well I spoke Spanish and English, and I had it all mixed up. It got so I couldn't talk either one. Finally, I just kept talking English and after a while she got used to it.

My mother called me an American. She says that first you've got to be loyal to your own race, and then to Americans. But I was practically *born* here, you know, so why can't I be an American? An American Puerto Rican?

Then, I don't go with Spanish girls much and she gets mad about that. I've got to say the truth about it. I don't tell her, but I like white girls better. White girls. I mean, did you ever see a Puerto Rican girl walk and talk? She looks like tomorrow the world is going to end and I better hurry home. But a white girl? She walks real slow. So slow.

I have Puerto Rican girl friends sometimes, but they are too old-fashioned. I mean, it's hard to say. See, like I have a sister. She's Puerto Rican, I'm Puerto Rican. But she's sort of like pure Puerto Rican. Her Puerto Rican ways are like from the old country. She believes the husband is ruler, that mostly what he says goes. She doesn't think she has to go to school, she only has to be a good housewife. Maybe, if I had a special kind of girl, I think a special kind of white girl, she wouldn't think so much about all that, she wouldn't think only about boyfriends. Maybe she'd talk about school, or politics, or some of that.

And that's what I want. Now, I want more. Oh, when I was thirteen, fourteen, all I wanted was to jump in a hall or behind the stairs and get from some girl what I wanted. Now, that's not it. I mean, if all you do is go outside and make love with a girl, you're not going to be interested for long. You can get anybody for that.

See, I'm not rich. I'm limited. But what I want is another kind of action.

Sometimes, I've been hanging around for a couple of weeks, and I get tired of nothing. Then, I get some work here and there, and maybe my father will give me a pound (a five-dollar bill) and then I take that money and I hit the night life. I like to see how the other kind behaves, what makes them different.

Take eating. You know a Puerto Rican eats practically all he can eat with his hands. Most of them do that. And when they eat with their forks, they don't know how to hold it. And dressing? Some Puerto Ricans like to dress up, too. But they don't have the same atmosphere. I mean, I *am* a Puerto Rican, and I dress like a Puerto Rican, because, I mean, there's no change. But—well—I guess I like the other style.

I guess I'd like to be like white people a little more than a Puerto Rican, although I am Puerto Rican. Not so much because they're different, it's because the Puerto Ricans have not learned this way yet. I mean they're still the same way. Whereas the whites, they have everything, so they can civilize themselves.

Sometimes I think it's the Puerto Ricans' own fault. Because I try to improve myself and, I mean, if I can try, they can do it, too.

I mean, the whole thing's mixed up. One time I think the Puerto Ricans don't ever get a chance to do anything. The Puerto Ricans and the coloreds, they're just stuck. Another time, I say, why don't they help themselves?

Me, I'm Puerto Rican, colored, and I'm not going to turn my back on that, but if you ask me, if I could say, "Which would you rather be?" Well, I mean, you've got to face it. I mean anybody would. If you ask me, which I'd rather be, well, man, I'd rather be white.

The one thing I'd like is to be finished with college and have all that worry behind me—all the difficulty of whether I'm going to get in, how my marks are going to be and all that over with. I'd like to be settled down in a good job with enough money to buy all the necessities and some luxuries. The thing I'd like is a lot of clothes, an awful lot of clothes. I love buying clothes. Then I'd buy a car if I were old enough and a house of my own and, of course, a dog. I see myself in a life with a lot of friends around me and a good family.

You look around and you see that there are some people who've made it and some who are certainly going to. Like my best friend has that kind of character. I don't know how to explain the way he is, but he is a very determined kind of person. Once he starts something, he can't put it down until he finishes it, and even though he is a lot of fun to be with, he really pays attention and works hard on what he is doing. Of course, like all my other friends, he wants to go to college. That's the important thing to us and to our families.

I admire my friend John, but the person in the world I admire most is my brother. I really think he's great. He's twenty-six and he's all set for life. He's got an answer for everything, for everything about life. He's got a good job, good standing in the community, a nice house, a beautiful car. My brother has everything he needs and he's got a wonderful personality, too. The thing about him is that he's very smart, but, more than that, he can handle difficult things. Nothing comes up in his life that my brother doesn't know the answer for and doesn't know how to take care of.

My mother would like to see my brother married and starting a family, but he wants to wait awhile. I think he's right, that twenty-seven or twenty-eight is a good time to get married. I see myself with two or three children whom I can take care of financially, physically, and in every way. And the kind of girl I'd want to marry would be well-mannered, respectable, and good-looking, with a good personality. The important thing is to have a refined girl who knows how to speak, act. My sister is like that. She might have come from any very wealthy home.

Then, after I'm settled, I never want to live anywhere but in New York. My father says that San Francisco is a great collection of the most comfortable people he has ever seen in his life. He says that there are very few poor people there and it's a wonderful city because of that, and almost as good as New York in other respects. Of course, he likes New York better and I really don't see moving myself, certainly not to the suburbs, where I'd have to travel back and forth all the time.

If I had enough money, I'd have a good house or apartment here in New York and a place in the country. I wouldn't like to have too much money, and if I did, I'd get rid of it through charities and that kind of thing. I guess I'd live pretty much like my parents do.

Then, I would bring my children up pretty much the way I've been brought up. I would protect them also in the same way that I've been protected. I know that kids like that bunch we nearly had a fight with think that we are over-protected, that we don't have as much freedom as they do. And it's true that my parents do protect me, and, in a sense, they always will protect me. They ask when I leave the house where I am going, when I am going to be back, whom I am going with. If they don't like where I am going, I don't go. I stay home.

But that's all. I am not in prison. I am free. I have my own life. They don't butt in, they help. I know that when they ask these questions or keep me from going certain places or doing certain things it's because they care for me—because they love me, and I'm grateful for that and I understand why.

A boy like those others isn't any more courageous than I would be in that situation. I mean if suddenly I were as poor as he is—all of a sudden in his situation—I would be terrified. But I would be able to work up to it and bear it as much as he can if I had the time to adjust to it. Then, I am not afraid to go out, to go wherever I like. I go out, I meet my friends, and we have a good time.

And we're not afraid of the girls, the way they think. We

have a lot of fun with them. Nice times, nice relationships. Now I don't think that a boy who has sex experiences when he's very young is going to be hurt by it. But I think that he is really too young and he should really be waiting. Then it's not as if that's the only way to get kicks out of life. In my family and with my friends, we're always laughing, always horsing around, having fun. More than they do, really.

Then, I think they grow up faster, but by the time we're all grown, most of us will have learned to take care of ourselves better. Just through experience we'll have learned ways of backing out, of picking the smartest way, the safest way to handle things. Even now, they're only braver than us because they've got a knife or a chain in their pocket. We don't lead a sheltered life at all. We lead a very well-backgrounded life. A better life, with a wider span of knowledge. I mean not only at school, but in all of life. In the rest of the city outside of this little neighborhood, we learn what to do with different problems that come up. I mean not all problems are fight problems —those, they can take care of better.

For example, if anything ever came up with the police, like the time my friend had trouble at the luncheonette, we could handle ourselves much better than they can. I know exactly what a policeman can do and what he can't do. The police see that and they leave us alone. More than that, the rest of the world respects us.

Then, the truth is, that the two Puerto Rican boys in our group aren't like that, or the couple of colored boys in our school. Even though their parents have to struggle to keep up with the tuition, they are just like us about fighting and knowing what's important. One of the Puerto Rican boys has a father who is even worse than mine as far as being strict goes. He watches his son's grades, he watches his homework, he watches everything his son does. He has a Spanish name and he can hardly speak English and his wife can't speak it at all, but he's a very smart man and he's decided that his boy is going to get in some college and that's all he thinks about. He is thinking ahead. Any time that boy gets a bad mark, he can't go out for a week.

Then, that boy in our gang who is a Puerto Rican is very

Ivy League. Really, the way he dresses, and the way he acts, and everything. He is really a lot of fun to be with, and he is a very nice guy. He brought a Puerto Rican girl to the last dance we had and she was very nice, too. She got along well with the other girls, was talking to them and doing well. She was quiet and she had good diction and was tall and beautiful. That boy goes to a good school and so does she, and it showed.

I think that if I knew some Puerto Rican girl like her, who was so refined and spoke so well, I might want to date her. I haven't done that yet and I'm not sure what my family would say. I'm really not. I think they'd leave it up to me and say, "If you really like her . . ." or something like that. But I've never done it.

There is a minority of those people who have those ideas and their kids are going to do better. The important thing is to give them the opportunity to get an education. You can't expect the Negro to be a sophisticated person without that. Like those awful people down South. I really can't stand them. Their leaders, they're really dumb men. They're white, but they *know* that the Negro is no good, that he is an animal. I think that those white men are really afraid of Negroes. They're afraid they're going to get together and rise up against the whites.

That's the trouble with all these demonstrations. There isn't any real segregation problem here in New York. Just from the neighborhood around where I live, I see there is almost none. But when you have all these demonstrations and all this tension, I think that the Negroes and the Puerto Ricans are really ruining their own chances. Everybody is fed up with all the demonstrations. I don't think its a good way to go about it. When they first started out, I thought it was a good idea, but now I see it's doing nothing; it's just hauling more police out, that's all.

I think that Negroes and Puerto Ricans realize that they're not getting all they should, and they want it bad enough, but they don't know how to get it. It's taking too long. It should have happened long ago for the Negroes, except they started out being considered slaves and that's hard to shake off. Puerto Ricans, they're a hard-working people if they have a good education, but I don't see any opportunity for them to get it because they're born on filthy streets, in rat-infested tenements and then they go to bad schools. For example, if they were put in a hard school, the kind that I've gone to, in first grade, I think they might learn to work hard and be trained in the right way. But if you put that kind of boy in a school like mine, right now, he wouldn't do anything.

The kind of schools that Puerto Rican and colored boys my age go to are much too easy. The kids make their own time, do what they want. The teachers can't do anything with them. They can give them homework, but the children can't be kept after school. They can't get punishment assignments overnight and they can't be hit. The teachers have no way to control them. They try to frighten them by failing them, but the boys don't care if they fail because they're not looking forward to college.

I don't know what they're looking forward to. I don't know. I've tried to figure it out when they sit on the stoops all day long, and I don't know. All summer you see them. What are they looking forward to?

I think it will take a long time, an awful long time for these people to pick themselves up. It's taking too long for it to work. Their whole life is fight. They're interested in building up a reputation and in a way it's the same thing as when the Irish came over. They were exactly the same way. But they knew how to go about it better. These people just don't understand what's going on, they don't really know.

For example, take all the excitement in New York about bussing children to school. I think it's just a lot of noise. I couldn't be bothered with this. I mean you see a picture of a mother crying over a child and it looks like a very good argument. But there is absolutely nothing wrong when a kid walks out of his house and walks into the school bus and is driven home. It's true he goes into a different neighborhood, but he doesn't get out of the bus five blocks away from the school. He gets out right at the door. It's the same for the whites and for the Negroes who are fighting that. I don't see anything wrong with it. I don't see why they fight it. In my neighborhood kids go on buses to private schools from the time they're in kindergarten.

Another example of using the wrong tactics was the riot they had in Harlem and other places around the country. I suppose there were some people, maybe a good proportion of them, that were really rioting because of what they feel about segregation. But I would say that very many were really out to get some loot. I was told a story that a CORE leader was saying that white people were looting and taking things. Then the day after, in the papers, there was a picture of a colored man in a full-length mink coat, a pocketbook, eight watches, carrying a bowling ball. Right there out on the street. When I see that, I know they're not rioting because of racial tension. I think they just want to get some loot.

I don't believe that even the incident that touched it off was legitimate. I kept saying to myself, if a colored man was a policeman, and he was on a street where troublemakers were, and a white boy came up to him carrying a knife, he wouldn't just stand there, he wouldn't just wait to be run through. I just couldn't see that. Because a whip, like that boy that was shot, was going wild and I know that if I were that policeman, I would have shot. Colored or no colored. I believe that the policeman shot for his hand and when the boy kept coming the policeman kept shooting. That's my feeling about it.

I'm against all this violence, against people like Malcolm X because if he says violence is what is going to beat the white man, he is not going to get anywhere. Because whether they are rioting in Harlem or in Rochester or anyplace else, they are just destroying themselves, because it's ruining their chances.

I think there's almost no discrimination in New York. Maybe some of the unions discriminate, but almost anywhere else in New York there are equal rights. I think that the trouble is that there is a real hate for the white man. A real hidden hate.

For example, Negroes can live anywhere they like in New York. I would feel terrible if a bum, a white bum, came to live in our apartment house with his family. I mean I wouldn't want a drunk or anyone who's noisy or ill-mannered to live there. I wouldn't want him, no matter what his color was. But if there were a respectable colored man, with a respectable family, I'd take him for sure. I don't think I'd even mind if there were seventeen or eighteen colored families in the building.

Maybe some of the older families, the older people in the building, would cause some trouble. But it would be some insignificant something which everyone would get over after a while. It would work out after a while. It would just take a little time.

But if I had my own method and I had enough power, I would have every child who said he was discriminated against put into a school, a good private school, if I had enough money. I'd put him in a school, I'd give him a great education and give him a background and a good home. Then he couldn't say that he was discriminated against and I'd show the rest of the people that there's nothing wrong with him. The white people could see that he was well backgrounded and a sophisticated person. All I can say is that someone who is respectable and refined and sophisticated is welcome in my house.

The important thing is the way parents are toward their children. How the parents care for their children, for their children's recreation, schools, what the parents do to help their child is the only thing that matters. I think that colored children have almost no help from their parents. They're not freerer than we are, they're in a real prison. They have to be taught everything in school because at home they learn nothing. I mean they have to be taught words like "good," simple things.

As for the parents, all they are interested in is whether the teachers discriminate against their children, whether they could get anything on the teacher for hurting their pride. They don't value education, because they never had any education themselves and they don't know what it's like. They don't understand that people can have a better life that way.

On the other side, I think those people would like to have a better life. Any one of them, any of the Puerto Rican boys, the tough guys in the neighborhood, he'd like to live as comfortably as we do. To have so many privileges. For example, we can go swimming at the private pool and they can't. I don't know why they can't, except they don't know anyone there. We have connections. Our parents belong to the club, or know people on the staff, so we can go there.

The other kids can swim in a public pool or go to the public-school gym, but they realize that we have more. The trouble is that what they do about it is all wrong. When we go to the pool, we always make sure that we keep our privilege. We keep to the rules, never make a racket, see that there are never too many of us in the corridors. We're careful to wash up before and not to run around the pool.

Well, about three days ago, about thirty of them came in a group with towels and bathing suits, right to the pool. We were in there, six of us, because we never go with more than six or eight at a time so that we don't take up too much room. Well, the members were using the pool when these kids ran in. They were stomping into the locker rooms and screaming and yelling, jumping off the diving board and throwing each other into the water. The life guard didn't know what to do. He looked around and he was bewildered. So Mr. Anderson, who runs that place, called the security guards and told them to get those boys out. If they had gone about it correctly, it might have been all right for them.

There's the same problem in church, at dances, or at clubs. Everybody is welcome and some Puerto Rican kids do come, but again, a lot of them do things the wrong way. For example, there's one priest that I like very much. He's a real nice guy and he feels sorry for them and tries to help them. But they don't want him. They won't pay attention to him and they tell him that. They say, "Get away from me."

He goes out into the street and he sees them. He goes over to talk to them, but if they don't respond, there is nothing he can do. It's not going to hurt him, but he feels sorry for them and can't help. Well, if they treat a priest like that, I don't think they're very nice.

I never see them at church, at Mass or at confession. Most of my friends were in the choir or altar boys when they were younger. Very few of the others ever were. I was in the choir for six years. Up until the time that my voice cracked. I loved the choir, I loved to hear the music. It's great.

I go to church every Sunday with my family and it's part

of the good feeling of security I have about my family. I enjoy the music, but I am really not the spiritual type. There is one boy in our parish whom everybody knows. He's an altar boy, all his life, and now he is a master on the altar. He went into the seminary for four years. He's very holy, pious, very nice. I think he really gets more out of church than I do, but I don't wish that I was more like him. I don't find a great interest in that kind of life. I like the music and I feel secure, and that's about all.

Two of the priests are very nice men and we often go and sit and talk with them all evening. We're very frank with them, but, for example, we wouldn't have told anybody there about that night we almost had the big fight. They wouldn't really understand and we'd be sort of looked down upon for being in that kind of predicament. We'd be considered instigators or something like that.

I don't mean to say that it's only Puerto Rican kids or colored kids who ever do anything wrong. I mean what makes me the most disgusted, no matter what color a person is, is someone who is always making stupid moves. What really destroys me is when a person who is about eighteen years old thinks and acts like a twelve-year-old. The kid I'm talking about is not very bright and he sometimes comes along to the movies with us. Once we went to a movie and he was watching and whenever a funny line came up and everyone else tittered quietly, he would guffaw and get up in his seat and whoop and then plop down. That destroys me.

Another incident like that, which really got me, happened a few weeks ago when I took a girl to a school dance. I only took her because she was my last resort, because she is very talkative and very giddy and I don't like that much. Well, after the dance a few of us went to a restaurant around the corner. I had on a raincoat that zips way up and as I was putting on the raincoat, she thought she would be really cute. She pulled the zipper up very hard and caught my neck in it. I was really furious. By the time I got it off my neck was bleeding and I was ready to pick up the table and throw it at the wall. I don't know how to explain this, but it really got me angry and I had all I could do to control myself. It was the closest I have ever come to exploding besides a few times on the football field when you can really get wild, when someone keeps clipping you, or when you keep getting your lumps with elbows in the mouth or something. Once, in that kind of game, I really saw red and my quarterback had to grab me by the neck and sit on me until I calmed down.

Most of the time though, I don't get that angry. Just sort of disgusted with something. And I don't get into any fights or serious trouble, because I try to avoid it. Even if I saw a fight or saw someone getting hurt, I'd stay away. If a gang of kids were beating up one boy, and I didn't know him, I'd wait until after they left and if the kid was hurt I'd help him. But I wouldn't want to get caught myself. I would not go over there like a fool and get myself killed. You can't do anything with the police in that sort of situation because they'd say it's my word against the word of a whole gang of boys. And I'd have to be a witness and that kind of trouble. I might try to get some adult who was standing around to help. But they feel the same way and would say that they didn't see it. They'd try to stay out of it themselves. Even my father told me one thing. He has said that if there is more than one of them, run. If there is one of you against one of them, and the other guy is the same size as you are, see what you can do, but don't ever try to take on more than you are.

I pretty much follow that advice. One time, though, some girls from our sister school were walking across the park and they were attacked by some rough colored girls. We just happened to walk through at the same time, after a parade we'd all been in, and we saw what was going on. Those colored girls were vicious. They were scratching and beating up the poor girls from the school, and our girls couldn't defend themselves. That time we really beat them off and escorted the girls to a taxi at the other end of the park.

All in all, though, very little of this sort of thing goes on in my own life. Pretty much, we go our own way, having a very good time, learning a lot, and preparing for life. Even when I think very hard, I wouldn't want to live anywhere else than where I live now. I love the block, the park, the neighbors. I am completely happy with my life. I've had a good life so far. Nothing dramatically wrong with it. Lots of laughs, lots of fun.